Be That Teacher

Be THAT Teacher

Rehumanizing Education with *Unapologetic Authenticity*

DWAYNE REED

Be That Teacher: Rehumanizing Education with Unapologetic Authenticity
© 2024 Dwayne Reed

All rights reserved. No part of this publication may be reproduced in any form or by any electronic or mechanical means, including information storage and retrieval systems, without permission in writing by the publisher, except by a reviewer who may quote brief passages in a review. For information regarding permission, contact the publisher at books@daveburgessconsulting.com.

> This book is available at special discounts when purchased in quantity for educational purposes or for use as premiums, promotions, or fundraisers. For inquiries and details, contact the publisher at books@daveburgessconsulting.com.

Published by Dave Burgess Consulting, Inc.
Vancouver, WA
DaveBurgessConsulting.com

Library of Congress Control Number: 2024946104
Paperback ISBN: 978-1-956306-87-3
Ebook ISBN: 978-1-956306-88-0

Cover and interior design by Liz Schreiter
Edited and produced by Reading List Editorial
ReadingListEditorial.com

*This book is dedicated to all the people who work
hard to see and treat other people as people.
Thank you! Oh, and it's for my scholars, too.
I love y'all, man!*

Contents

Intro 1
Chapter 1: Do You, Fam 11
Chapter 2: Rebel against the Norm 23
Chapter 3: Relationships Matter 43
Chapter 4: Gather the Real Data 57
Chapter 5: How Do You See Me? 71
Chapter 6: Let Kids Be Kids. 87
Chapter 7: The Teacher as the Lead Learner 101
Chapter 8: It Takes a Team to Teach 117
Chapter 9: Everyone Deserves Your Excellence 139
Chapter 10: Teaching beyond the Classroom 155
Outro 169

Acknowledgments 177
About Dwayne Reed 179
More from Dave Burgess Consulting, Inc. 180

Intro

*I*f I slipped up, even half a step, I was going down. And I knew it. I was in the fourth grade at a small school. I was charismatic and outgoing but self-conscious. Although I liked to chat, I knew when to turn it off. I wasn't talkative to the point of being disruptive. But this day in the fourth grade stands out in my mind as the first time I got "in trouble" at school.

My teacher didn't like me and I could tell. Kids just know these things. It was like the teacher had beef with me—a nine-year-old!—and was always putting extra scrutiny on me. I felt policed and patrolled in her classroom. My every word and action were being watched.

On this occasion, our class was going over our spelling words. I looked up at the wall to see what time it was, probably bored out of my mind. That was it—I didn't speak or do any silly dance. No disruption. I just looked. But after I checked the clock, my fourth-grade teacher, Mrs. Jansen,[1] stopped everything and stared at me. I had my erasable pen in my mouth, I remember. Just chewing on stuff. A kid.

She stopped teaching to fix me with her stare, and all of my classmates saw that she was watching me pointedly. There was a brief silence, then my peers began to laugh. *Now* there was a disruption in her class. When they laughed, she frowned. She got so mad that she stopped the entire lesson to write me a detention slip and send me to the principal's office.

---

1 I've changed the names in this book to preserve individuals' anonymity.

I was holding back my tears as Mrs. Jansen gave me that detention slip. I had never been in that kind of trouble before, so I had no idea what to expect. It was scary. The moment I walked out that door, I began to cry my heart out. Gasping for air. Dry heaving. Eyes red and heavy. Ever since I was little, I would turn things over and over in my mind until I could figure out the reason those things happened. I couldn't understand this one. That detention slip made no sense to me. Why was the name Dwayne Reed written there? And for allegedly disrupting the class? I hadn't done anything.

My teacher's beliefs about me created a situation where there wasn't one.

It felt like the longest walk of all time down that hallway to see Mrs. Hurts—the principal. When I walked into her office, our school leader immediately recognized my emotions. "Dwayne, what's going on?" she asked. "Are you okay? I don't typically see you this way." Whereas Mrs. Jansen saw me as a troublemaker and was always waiting to catch me doing bad, Mrs. Hurts saw me as the good kid. I could feel it. Kids just know these things.

But there was something uncharacteristic about me that day, and she knew it. She was empathetic to me. She saw my humanity.

After telling her my side of things, I said my stomach hurt, so she handed me a peppermint. After I calmed down some, she said, "We're going to get to the bottom of this." And I believed her. Mrs. Hurts asked me to walk up to the classroom with her. Out of sheer nerves, I accidentally swallowed the peppermint whole, so I asked if I could get some water at the fountain on the way. I drank for so long, she joked, "Make sure to leave some for the fish." Her humor comforted me.

When we went back to my classroom, Mrs. Hurts requested that Mrs. Jansen step out briefly to explain what happened. Despite Mrs. Hurts's kindness, I still had to serve the detention. Not exactly the fairy-tale ending I hoped for. But that day has always stuck out to me as an example of the two different outlooks you can have on students. You can believe that kids are bad and that you will eventually catch them doing bad; or you can believe that kids are human and choose to see the good in them.

My fourth-grade teacher just knew I was up to no good.

My school's principal just knew there was good in me.

Of the two choices, which kind of educator would you want in your life? Which one would you have wished for as a child? Which one are you choosing to be? For me, the answer is clear. I always err on the side of grace and look for goodness. I am thirsty to discover the things that would make any parent or caregiver proud of their child. And I imagine that's the teacher you want to be.

Well, be *that* teacher!

While it would be oversimplifying things to say that specific day began my career as an educator, it is certainly a day I look back on when I begin to trace how my philosophy on education began. But, as with any career, the path has been long to get to where I am.

> **I am thirsty to discover the things that would make any parent or caregiver proud of their child.**

• • • •

If you've picked up this book, chances are you've seen one of my viral music videos or heard of my reputation as America's Favorite Rapping Teacher. I have enjoyed great success in teaching and have been lucky enough to have that success open up a world of opportunities for me. It's led me to *Good Morning America* and being able to fulfill my dreams of being in some of the world's most renowned recording studios and on some of its most impressive stages. But if you looked for the origins of all that success, you might not see a natural, obvious path between where I started and where I am today.

The truth is I stumbled into the education profession. I was originally studying for a business management degree at Purdue University.

But I couldn't afford the tuition to finish my degree, so I dropped out of school and got a job at a home improvement store back in Chicago. One evening after work, I took an online aptitude test. All my results kept telling me I should work in some sort of social service—nursing, counseling, therapy, teaching. I can't do blood, so nursing was off the list. But the aptitude test was on to something! It started to dawn on me: I should teach. What's more about helping people than helping young minds grow and develop?

I searched Google for "day in the life of a teacher" and "day in the life of a Black, male teacher." I scoured YouTube. I soaked up all the options, enrolled in a local community college, and got my associate's degree. Around that time, there was a Chicago Public Schools teacher strike. Teachers were fighting for fair pay, among other things, and the kids who relied on schools for meals or a place to go during the day were going to be in a tough spot. Sympathizing with them, I found my way to a program connected to a Christian ministry that was housing and tutoring students who needed help during the strike. Finally, it felt like something I could do that would truly make a difference in people's lives.

I went once a week to Club, as it was called, and started to develop relationships with the kids. When the strike ended, I kept going back to Club. By the summer, those in charge had been impressed enough with my work that they offered me a paid position as summer camp coordinator. I couldn't have been more thrilled. And I blossomed in that role. It felt like putting on a lively, fun performance every day. I not only worked with children but also interacted with all the groups involved, a coalition of churches and ministries, to make sure they all had what they needed. I helped with discipline, too, although even back then it was my own brand. I was having restorative conversations with kids before I even knew what restorative conversations were.

I tried to be the person who spoke to kids the way I wished people would have spoken to me. "What happened?" "How can I help?" "What did you learn from this?" "How can we fix this together?" "What can we do to move forward?" I wanted every person who interacted with me to feel like they truly got what they needed from me.

I was in that role for two summers, and it was an amazing growth opportunity. Being camp coordinator built my capacity for running a successful program, and I learned the value of a team in creating initiatives that empower and uplift kids.

Eventually, I wanted a four-year degree, but one that wouldn't put me in decades of debt. So I transitioned to Eastern Illinois University. By that point, I was excited as ever about teaching as a profession, and it was affirming to hear my professors tell me, "You've got it, whatever 'it' is." Teaching as a profession felt right in a way that other attempts had not. It was at EIU that I saw a video in one of my gym classes of a math teacher introducing himself to his new students in song.

I'd grown up a small, self-conscious, shy, insecure kid. But I knew that I could sing and rap. I listened to "Kick, Push," a song by Lupe Fiasco about skateboarding, and remixed it to be all about basketball. Music was a thing I had enjoyed doing for a long time, but I never performed for anyone. I might rap for my homies at the lunch table, but I never kept it going beyond that. I couldn't be a rapper. I didn't have the look. I didn't have the style or the swagger. I thought my voice was too small. In short, I didn't think of myself a rapper, but I considered myself someone who rapped.

Despite all of that, I wrote my own introductory rap then planned to premiere my first music video for the kids I was teaching at the time. I didn't expect it to be anything much. I just wanted to connect with my scholars and to present myself in a fun, light-hearted way they could relate to. I knew a guy who did videography, so he came to the school and filmed the video in one take. We didn't map anything out or make a detailed plan. We didn't search for the perfect backdrop. He just brought his camera to school and filmed me rapping my song. He edited it, and I uploaded it to social media the next day.

Pretty soon, it was highlighted on the local news. Then, it went viral. Then *Good Morning America* called.

This wasn't a video I'd created thinking, "Maybe this will bring me to national prominence." It wasn't something I knew was going to go viral. The heart behind the video was that I wanted my fourth graders to think, "This person really rocks with me. This teacher cares about me."

Being on *Good Morning America* was surreal and exhilarating! At 6:00 a.m., I was ready to go! On-air, I hit all the points I wanted to make, and I was excited that my way of interacting with the kids was striking a nerve across the country.

In my interview, I mentioned Ron Clark, the superstar educator and *New York Times* bestseller. Immediately after my appearance, Mr. Clark reached out on social media. It was cool that I could talk to a person who was making such a difference in education. I was reminded of the passage in Proverbs which says, "Your gifts will make room for you and bring you before great people."[2]

Gaining a national brand on *Good Morning America* happened amazingly and unexpectedly fast. It was exhilarating and fun, and so many other opportunities came as a result of that experience. More media folks reached out to me. Teacher websites gave me education gifts. My social media following grew. And I started to share ideas and interact with people doing great things and making big moves in education and other fields.

As I began my career in education, I kept using a mix of my own instincts and the latest scholarly research in education and psychology to understand what helps students, teachers, and communities thrive. Over time, I developed a system that works. You'll find it in these pages. Some of it may sound intuitive. Some of it may challenge you. When I say, "This is what works," I'm not suggesting this is the only thing that works; it just works for me. As you'll read in this book, I am always a work in progress, as I believe we should all be. With this book, I am giving you the best that I have right now. I offer it because I want other

---

2 Prov. 18:16.

people to have the same joy and success I've been blessed to experience. If you read my ideas and they help make one of your days better than the last one, I've won. And you've won.

These days, one of the labels I have is educational influencer. I get a bunch of likes on social media, and people book me as a keynote speaker at their events. Cool stuff! But the best moments come from my scholars and their adults.

I'm reminded of a time years ago when I lived next to a barber shop. One of my former students was going to the shop for a haircut. When he spotted me on the street, his mouth gaped, his breath making a little cloud in the cold air. He ran out of the car to hug me with a huge grin across his face. "That's Mr. Reed!" he called out to his dad, so excited. It was like he'd seen his favorite celebrity. He'd been my student years before and was in the seventh or eighth grade by that point when kids are supposed to be in their "cool" phase. But he looked at me as if I was the coolest guy on the block. That felt better than *Good Morning America*. Not because I need to be recognized, but because his enthusiasm meant that I'd made a lasting impression on him.

> If you read my ideas and they help make one of your days better than the last one, I've won. And you've won.

Chances are you've had experiences like this, too. Being a teacher means we have the opportunity to impact so many more lives than the average person. Not all of us may be able to get on *Good Morning America*, but we can all be a star to our kids by giving them grace and making them feel loved. I have always felt called to widen my circle of influence by doing more than teaching my kids, but by also empowering educators, parents, and everyone who has an interest in the future. If I empower other teachers, I can help reach so many more children than I could ever teach in the classroom alone.

My message is not mine alone. I'm not the creator of some of this information. It's built through my experience in the classroom and in life, as well as the data about what's working today, some of which contradicts old ideas that many teachers hold.

We all have a superpower. One of mine is that I can speak in a manner that's bold, undeniably truthful, and authentic. I'm not afraid to ruffle feathers for the good of our profession and to rehumanize people. That's what I think makes my message mine.

What I'm Hoping You'll Get Out of This Book

My intentions for you are twofold. I'm hoping you can leave with practical strategies to put into place immediately in your own classroom, with your own children, or in your own life. But more broadly, my hope is that you'll have a positive change of heart. If this book caught your attention, chances are that we already see eye to eye in a lot of ways. I'm honored you'll give my sometimes-unorthodox ideas a chance to see if they fit with your toolbox of teaching and classroom management strategies. I also want you to look deep within yourself to see what unique gifts you bring to the classroom. It's crucial to engage in professional development, but I want this book to empower you to be authentically you. Please ask yourself this question: What is the good in me that no one could stop me from putting out into the world? That's what's going to make the world better and brighter!

Because ultimately, that's what it's about—making the world a brighter place. We often hear about the negativity in the world, on the news, or in our neighborhoods. The happy stuff rarely makes the headlines. But those good, happy, wholesome, humanity pieces are the only things that can ever counterbalance the darkness we're hoping to drive away. I'm not naïve about the challenges we face. But I truly believe love, intentionality, and embracing humanity can radically change the world. That's what I'm about, and I hope we can be partners in this endeavor. Let's do this! Be *that* teacher!

Hello, I'm your teacha'

My name's Mr. Reed, and
it's very nice to meet ya

I'm from Chicago,
I love eating pizza

And I dress to impress,
but I still rock sneakers

CHAPTER 1

Do You, Fam

*I*f you've heard of me before picking up this book, it's probably because of my classroom rap called "Welcome to the 4th Grade" that went viral. My spontaneous classroom raps are a highlight of my teaching style that I am well known for among my scholars, too. I like to think of myself as America's favorite rapping teacher. I grew up in hip-hop culture (think Lil Wayne, Kanye West, Lupe Fiasco) and find wisdom and inspiration whenever head-bobbing beats line up with fire lyrics. That's me, authentically, and I bring that to the classroom every day.

In this chapter, I'm going to make the case for why it's critical for you as an educator to *do you*, which means bringing the deepest things about who you are to your interactions with young people. In whatever ways you shine the most and however you feel most comfortable showing up, that is what I'm encouraging you to do and to be, consistently.

What makes you *you*? What sets you apart from everyone else in the game, even if it might seem different or a little strange? Or what's something that's considered common or basic, but you still really like it? Go ahead and express *that*! In your classroom, be loud with it, be bold with it. Be confidently you, not some robot, by-the-book, straight-from-the-university teacher or what the system thinks a teacher should be. Bring *you* to the table. Shoot, bring your own table!

That's what makes things fun, exciting, and enjoyable for everyone in education.

We All Appreciate Authenticity

Looking back, I only enjoyed school when I enjoyed the teacher. When the human in front of me was cool in their own way, I was cool spending time in front of them. Even if the subject material wasn't interesting to me, a dope teacher being their natural self could make it all worthwhile. Science began to click because my biology teacher used to be a professional baseball player and would tell us stories about his time in the league, which kept us engaged. AP Economics made sense to me because "Mr. Macro vs. Micro" was absolutely hilarious! As educators, we owe it to our students to make those 185 days of school as meaningful as possible, and we can only accomplish that task when we tell our kids meaningful things about ourselves.

Have you ever seen a performance at an open mic night that you weren't expecting to like, but it totally blew your mind? Maybe it was a techno-polka group, or opera, or spoken word, but the performers were überconfident in themselves and simply did *their* thing! Even if it wasn't exactly your cup of tea, at the end of the day, it was still great stuff. That's exactly how teachers can show up for our students—confident in our coolness and in how we carry ourselves. Let's rock the house out, I say! We owe it to kids, and we owe it to ourselves to be ourselves.

> **We owe it to kids, and we owe it to ourselves to be ourselves.**

But back to the rap—maybe you're not as confident in your rap bars, or your pen game ain't as strong as your favorite hip-hop star. I don't see that as a problem. Despite any lack of rhythm or dope poetry skills, every teacher should still be a rapper.

Now you might be thinking, "C'mon, Mr. Reed. I listen to country, alternative rock, and gospel. I am *not* a rapper." I hear that, but it doesn't matter who you are, where you're from, or what you typically listen to—you belong in front of your classroom's microphone. You've just gotta embrace your inner star.

If you haven't caught on yet, I'm using the term *rapper* as a metaphor. Maybe you're a line dancer or an introvert. Maybe you collect and trade rare postage stamps, or you're a bookworm who runs a social media account about Gothic romance. Whatever you are at your core or whatever makes you go, that's exactly what you need to touch the lives of those you serve. That's real rap, and the real is what people feel. We all appreciate authenticity. So even as a teacher, be a rapper. Or in other words, just be you. Do you, fam.

Rapping is my superpower—what's yours?

A Few Questions to Think About

What causes or activities do you spend a lot of time thinking about, donating to, or giving your energy to?

If you asked your friends to describe you by a few ideas or mottos, what answers would they give? (Ask your friends and family for ideas here.)

What is a rule you live by that you never break? I've heard answers ranging from the Golden Rule to making a point of dancing every day. Everyone's answer is unique.

> If you only had one day left alive, and all the health and money in the world, how would you spend that day? In other words, what matters most to you?
>
> _____
>
> _____

I need teachers to know that *we* are the asset. Our presence alone adds value to the space we occupy with our scholars, and everything else we express about ourselves is icing on the cake. Once all is said and done, what in particular will your scholars miss most about you? What will they remember about you? What little quirks will your staff cherish about you? How will you choose to show up? How will you tell the people in your life who you are? How will you make sure they will have always had someone real to connect with? Answering these questions is what it means to "do you."

Put It on Display

We need to make sure that information about ourselves is readily available to our kids. They shouldn't have to search high and low to learn things about the person they spend so much time with. So, teachers, go out of your way to share with your kids every cool experience, interest, insight, and idea that says something about who you are. As an educator, one of the easiest things you can do to foster a positive relationship with the people in front of you is to talk about yourself. What's appealing about you? What makes you human in their eyes? What can a five-year-old, a fifteen-year-old, or a fifty-five-year-old look at and say, "Oh, me too!"? Talk about your background, your hobbies, your family, your hopes, and your dreams. Those kinds of things will draw them in and keep them coming back for more.

Like most curious kids, my fifth graders would often ask me about my marital status. They couldn't understand how I was still single, which I could definitely appreciate. One day during recess, while talking to a few of my scholars, one of them said, "Mr. Reed, you need you a girlfriend!" I said, "You know what? I do!" My kids laughed at my excitement! Playfully I asked, "Would you happen to know any women that I should hit up? Are they looking for their very own Venti Mocha Cookie Crumble Frappuccino of a man who has a steady job, great benefits, and a car?"

Immediately, KiKi—the one who told me I needed a girl in the first place—looked me up-and-down with one of the funkiest of faces and said, "Uh, no! I would *never* link you with anybody I know, Mr. Reed." She then came with the knockout, saying, "You ugly!" And when kids say things like that, they mean it. So I walked away with my head down, knowing that I'd probably never find love. But several years later, that same student was at my wedding to the woman of my dreams. Kiki was even asking her mama if she could stay longer because she was having so much fun! Guess I'm not that ugly after all, am I?

The point is this: our kids want to be a part of our lives. Let them! They're curious about us, and we have a great opportunity to tell them about ourselves. Does this mean I only spend time talking to students about my personal life? Of course not. There's serious learning going on in my classroom.

My teaching style is not focused solely on standing at the front of the classroom talking about myself or rapping all day. There's a balance. I look for the right moment to discuss my life, then I fall back. I let my kids ask questions, I answer them truthfully, and then we're back to business. Of course, I'm mindful of what I say and how much, but, otherwise, it's fine. Connecting on an interpersonal level is a part of learning. Our kids are not just learning math and language arts, they're learning how to engage with adults and their peers in a safe, curious, and conscious way.

Share Your Heart

Every minute spent influencing young people is a privilege. Anyone drawn to this profession already knows that, but the system can often grind this basic truth out of us. Over time, we can start to forget that this job is truly heart work—the drive that we have to serve comes from within our heart and is used to touch the hearts of others. It's my hope that reading about my experiences can help you excavate the unique things you bring to the classroom and embolden you to share them with your students. I promise you—this will multiply your joy!

Studies increasingly point out that teachers showing up authentically and sharing thoughts and emotions leads to better outcomes for kids and teachers.[1] "Teachers who felt connected with their students were more likely to report joy and less frequently anxiety and anger. In accordance with attachment theory,[2] positive interpersonal relationships reflect security and, thus, do not only play an important role for students, but appear to function as antecedent of teachers' emotional wellbeing as well."[3]

I love getting to show my scholars who I am, how I'm human, and the ways in which they can help me. Showing them these parts of myself connects them to me and makes my work and our shared classroom experience feel real. Feel alive! Giving them an inside look at my life gives me at least twenty to thirty more chances for another human being to speak life into me. Just because they're kids doesn't mean they can't help. When I choose to see the best in them and give them the chance to see the best in me, that connection becomes unbreakable; the fruit of this connection is truly amazing. When we share our heart with everyone, everyone's hearts can grow.

---

1 Gerda Hagenauer, Tina Hascher, and Simone E. Volet, "Teacher Emotions in the Classroom: Associations with Students' Engagement, Classroom Discipline and the Interpersonal Teacher-Student Relationship," *European Journal of Psychology of Education* 30, no. 4 (March 15, 2015): 385–403, https://doi.org/10.1007/s10212-015-0250-0.

2 Jude Cassidy and Phillip R. Shaver, *Handbook of Attachment: Theory, Research, and Clinical Applications*, 2nd. ed. (New York: Guilford Press, 2008).

3 Hagenauer, Hascher, and Volet, "Teacher Emotions in the Classroom."

For Those Who Don't Need to Be Liked, Just Respected

Before we go any further, let's address the objections you have or have heard about exhibiting this kind of authenticity in the classroom. First, "How do you maintain respect?"

When people hear words such as *fun* or *likable* or *laughter*, especially those of the old guard, they think disrespect will be at an all-time high. "Don't let them see you smile until Christmas" is an adage you've most likely heard. People who subscribe to this line of thinking believe kids will walk all over them if they're anything less than a drill sergeant. Well, I'm here to tell you that nothing could be further from the truth. Respect doesn't come from being stern or stiff. Respect comes from being firm, fair, and flexible. Respect also comes from holding yourself and your scholars to high standards, giving them your excellence, and expecting theirs. Above all, authenticity produces respect. No matter who you are, if you're generally kind and genuinely you, kids will respect you.

It's impossible for me not to be the fun-loving, goofy guy who tells corny jokes and tries to dance. That's who I am, and my kids appreciate it. I'm being real. I'm being me, and they enjoy that. While they probably can't stand my jokes, they would surely come to my show in a heartbeat if I ever did stand-up comedy. While they don't like my dancing, they like *me* dancing. To quote the great Rita Pierson, "Kids don't learn from people they don't like." What have you given them to like about you? If they don't like you, chances are they aren't learning anything from you! That said, it's okay if your students enjoy you. And yes, even if they like you!

Another objection I hear is, "I don't have the time to try to be enjoyed by my students or liked by them. I don't have time to build those kinds of relationships with over five hundred kids." There's no doubt that a career in education is as challenging as it's ever been, with shifting requirements, changing curricula, and added pressures from parents and administrators. These challenges are real. The recommendation still stands, however. I'm not suggesting that you spend your thirty-minute class trying to get your kids to like you. I'm suggesting that you take half an hour to be the real you and simply watch how many kids become amazed by you.

"Do you" does not mean do more. "Do you" means be you.

One of the other objections I hear from fellow educators is that we've been trained to not get too personal with kids. It's possible your teacher prep courses, colleagues, or administrators told you getting too personal would be a bad idea. That's understandable. Not everything is appropriate to share with kids, and we must be as cautious as possible to protect the most vulnerable among us. And if we're keepin' it real, you technically don't have to share anything at all. You have a right to privacy and to share only what you're comfortable sharing. But one thing I know for certain is that revealing details about ourselves can help form human connections. Information is a pathway to empathy. The more a person knows, the more grace, compassion, care, and understanding they'll have the ability to show.

You don't have to share your deepest, darkest fears. But, if you are afraid of the dark, some of your kids might respect you a bit more after learning that. If you love crochet, a few students might think that's *sew* cool and might even want to join you in creating something crafty to wear! Tell them stuff about yourself.

One quick and important note: you can be relatable, likeable, warm, caring, welcoming, friendly, and every other positive synonym under the sun, but that doesn't mean you have to be friends with your students. *Set boundaries.* Kids do not need their teachers to try to be their friend. They have friends. They need you to be their teacher, to be *that* teacher.

To go back to an example of something I share with my students—my passion for rap music—I'm not saying that every one of us should be recording music and putting it out for the world to hear. That would be tragic. And I'm not saying that we should all dress, act, and speak like what we think hip-hop culture is. That would definitely be tragic. And most importantly, you do not have to be Mr. Reed! Let me be Mr. Reed. You be you!

What's *your* big thing? What are you confident showing off? My thing is rap, so best believe I'ma rap! I pay homage to the greats then borrow components from hip-hop to help frame my pedagogy and connect with my kids. But maybe you already bring some of this into your own work. Maybe you've already tapped into your inner rapper.

Do you engage the crowds (your scholars) with your wordplay and delivery (your instruction)? Have you used call-and-response techniques as attention grabbers? Do you ever put on a persona when you hit the stage (your classroom) that completely consumes you and excites the crowd? Have you acted as a hype man, cheering loudly when your students have produced excellent work or said something great? Have you ever read poetry in class or told a mathematics joke with a hilarious punchline? If you answered yes to any of those questions, you, my friend, have been doing your rap thizzle.

Maybe you're not going to get a record deal anytime soon. Maybe you can't stay on beat to save your life. Even if that's the case, keep facilitating the rhythm of your classroom with your words, actions, and performance. Embrace your inner rapper. Do you, fam.

Reflections

Which characteristics or qualities of yours make you *you*? Which of these are you most proud of? Which of these would you like to share more about with your students?

_____

_____

_____

What is something you like or do outside of the classroom that you can bring to your work to help students see you in a brighter light? What connections can you use to help inspire them? What ways can "outside you" motivate "inside them"?

_____

_____

_____

To many kids, all teachers seem and sound the same. What's something you bring to the classroom that only your students get to experience and be proud of? What do your scholars have bragging rights over?

_____

_____

_____

Many kids won't come out of their shell until they see others do so. What can you say or do to help make kids more comfortable being their authentic selves?

_____

_____

_____

The beauty and brilliance of everyone's true self is amazing! Can you think of ways that being your most authentic self makes the workplace a better place for others? For your staff mates? For your administration? For yourself?

_____

_____

_____

Sometimes, you gotta say No,
stand up, and fight back

Even if they hate it and
exclude you from the pack

Rebel against the norm
if the norm is not fair

Yes, fight for anyone,
any time, and anywhere!

CHAPTER 2

Rebel against the Norm

People who knew me growing up might chuckle at the fact that I've got a chapter in my book that advocates for rebelling. Dwayne Reed, a rebel? No way! I was as big of a Goody Two-shoes as they come. By-the-book, cookie-cutter, follow the rules to a T. My mama put that righteous fear of God in me (if you know, you know), and I just knew how to play the school game: don't talk in class, do your work, play nice at recess, laugh at the teacher's jokes, and never buck against the system in any way. I was shy as a kid, and although I had dreams of becoming a big musical artist, I didn't draw attention to myself. And I certainly didn't rebel.

But as a classroom teacher, I rebel against many rules and policies that I don't believe serve my scholars or myself. Here are some examples: I never take away recess from a kid—how dare I strip away a crucial aspect of their humanity just because I might have felt disrespected by them or because they didn't get some work done? I never give zeroes on anything—why would I want my students to fail? I never stick to the pacing guide—how can people who have never seen or taught my kids tell me where we should be in our learning? I never take work home—it's gonna be there tomorrow, so that's when I'll get to it. I refuse to practice punitive disciplinary measures with my kids. Sure, give logical consequences that hold them accountable! But why not show them grace and have restorative conversations instead of "teaching them a lesson"? These are just a few ways in which I rebel daily in school, and I hope educators reading this book will feel empowered to follow suit.

Look, I am not suggesting that we rock the boat just for boat rockin's sake. Rebellion can point to selfish ambition, pride, and a hardened heart. Doing your own thing just for the sake of doing it ain't how you spose' to do it, fam. Let me be abundantly clear—rebellion for its own sake is wrong.

However, I'm shouting to anyone who will listen: let's get into this education game and rebel! I use that word because it's meant to wake people up and stir the pot in a way that infuses our work with fiery seasonings and herbs. In other words, let's get spicy, y'all!

According to Merriam-Webster, rebellion means opposition to one in authority or dominance. When things are going well and those in authority are representing our interests as they should, rebellion isn't necessary. But when things aren't what they should be, discussion and negotiation is often the best way to achieve change. But sometimes, downright rebellion is required. That time has come in education.

Rebelling in Schools

The fight for schools means not being afraid to get into trouble when you're pursuing the best interests of your students. I don't mind going against the grain when I recognize that the trouble I might get into could bring about better situations or services for my kids. Civil rights leader and US Representative John Lewis, may he rest in continued peace, said, "Get in good trouble. Necessary trouble." I can't think of another time in our history where that call was more appropriate.

Now is when we rebel against schools being testing and data centers instead of learning centers.

Now is when we rebel against the powers that be who constantly put more and more work on teachers' plates.

Now is when we rebel against treating students and staff like robots instead of the beautiful human beings they are.

Teachers *should* be getting into "good trouble." We should be committed to trying new things or doing old things in a new way. Rebelling, in this context, means switching up the flow no matter who loved or benefitted from the old approach. If the new wave protects or provides for more people—or is more inclusive—ride that wave 'til kingdom come.

Above all, rebelling in schools means not being afraid to ask "why" when faced with a policy, procedure, or when someone says, "It's just the way we do things." We can no longer just sit around and accept everything thrown our way. Instead, we should all become like curious kids and question everything!

Rebel in Your Own Way

To be clear, you are not a bad teacher if you choose not to rebel in any of the ways I suggest. Everyone's got their thing or their own motivation. Listen to what moves you. You don't have to do this work in any particular way, but I am suggesting that you do this work in your own way. In other words, do you, but do something.

It's also possible to be a rule follower and a rebel at the same time. Don't let folks tell you differently. In fact, I'd consider myself to be both. Sure, I want people to get fired up about changing education, but I don't just want to burn it all down. I'm not a radical, I'm a rebel. There's a difference. Rebellion in educational spaces should be viewed as good and needed. Causing waves that can wash away injustice or exclusion is a blessed calling. It is okay for you to follow the rules, but it is equally okay to rebel against the ones that suck, when necessary. Find out what good and necessary trouble looks and feels like for you, then get down to business.

Practical Ways to Rebel in the Classroom

While rebelling against the norm can make enormous change, it doesn't always have to be a gargantuan task. There are daily, practical ways of rebelling. For example, if I'm reading a chapter of a book to my scholars and they're deeply engaged in the story, I may keep reading when I'm supposed to be rolling over into my science or social studies block. Or, if you're sharing a story from your life during geometry that's got everyone hanging onto your every word, finding x can wait. Keep those kids captivated. These are small but significant opportunities to rebel.

Don't be afraid to abandon a lesson whenever you get the opportunity to teach a life lesson. That's good trouble! The lessons you don't plan are often the ones that kids remember. Taking ten minutes off from math or reading one day will not cause the world to end, but it might fill the world with more engaged learners.

Broadly, rebelling entails thinking critically about what we've decided to normalize. Normal according to whom? To serve what population? To what end? If it's normal to insist that children be quiet most of the day, who is that for? Is that for the kids' benefit or the adults'?

A thousand questions like these could be considered in a day, and a million during a school year. If things work, by all means, let them continue to work. But if there can be a better, more effective path to travel, let's take that one. When we question the norm from the jump, we participate in the disruption and uprooting of archaic and harmful policies and attitudes. Schools have a lot of those, so why not work to rid our spaces of them? This challenging work done on the front end benefits everyone on the back end. That is why educational rebellion is needed. This is why *you* should rebel.

Questions to Ask When Rebelling

The key to rebelling against the norm is to ask questions. When did we start doing things this way? Why did we make that shift? Who stands to gain from this? Who, if anyone, will this adversely affect?

Concepts like rules around how much sound kids can make, how they should move (or not move) their bodies, where they can go, or how they can engage with their schoolwork are all fair game for inquiry. If a rule is helping scholars have a better experience, great! But if you're finding that your students are constantly bumping up against a specific rule or norm, "getting into trouble" over a rule, or a norm is taking away from their experience, that's the rule or norm to ask questions about. Consider the following:

Maybe hats should be OK to wear in class.

Maybe the volume of our students' voices doesn't have to be on level zero in the hallways or during lunch.

Maybe homework shouldn't be assigned in elementary and middle schools (and maybe not even in high school).

Maybe grades shouldn't be *A* through *F*.

Maybe teachers should be encouraged to play more games, watch more movies, and take more breaks with their scholars.

Rebel against "Every Instructional Minute Matters"

I've taught in several schools where the push has been to consider that "Every instructional minute matters." It's this idea that not a single moment of the school day should be "wasted" by not teaching something academic. Within this model, every second must be filled with busywork, activities, teaching, academic engagement, and "learning." It's an early-1900s factory model. Bell-to-bell. No reasonable breaks. Very little fun. And if you do get a break, you'd better keep it quick, then get back to work! Lunch is just twenty minutes, and recess might be fifteen short minutes with no balls or playground materials. And that's if students even get a recess. It's miserable!

I was once a middle school social studies teacher. At that job, students in sixth through eighth grade were not allowed to go outside during their school day. Even if their teacher felt it was appropriate, all work had been completed, and the weather was nice, the autonomy to take students out was not there. Any form of recess would need to have been requested then approved before permission to go outside was granted. It felt real prison-like.

Because I was an educational rebel—and just a decent human being—I often took my scholars outside regardless of this policy. Apparently, that didn't sit well with the leadership team, so one day, I was summoned into a meeting with my administrators to discuss why I was breaking this rule.

I wanted to say, "Because I'm a human and I have a heart." Instead, I said, "Because these are kids, and their work is finished, so they deserve to go outside and play." I rebelled and confidently shared my thoughts and principles with my principal. Unfortunately, she resisted and responded, "Well, this is how it's going to go *here*."

Soon after, I was no longer *there*.

Five days before my eighth graders were set to graduate, I got fired from my position as their social studies teacher. It was right after their graduation practice when I took them outside to the school's playground. Two minutes into enjoying freedom, fresh air, and our holistic educational experience, an administrator rushed out of the building and angrily ordered my class to return inside.

"Why do we need to go in?" I asked. "They have five days of school left, and they're finished with all of their work. Instruction has stopped. Can't we just celebrate their accomplishments and enjoy the nice weather?" I questioned.

"Did you ask the principal?" the administrator replied.

"No," I said. "And I shouldn't have to! These are kids who deserve to be outside! Do we need permission to be human? Do we need permission to be free?"

At this school, and many others, the unfortunate answer to these questions is "Yes."

Humanity doesn't reign; the time card does. The checklist is king. Policies and board-mandated practices are seemingly more important than people.

Let me be brutally honest with you—there *can* be consequences to rebelling. I've experienced them firsthand. It's not always pretty being a rebel, and oftentimes, there can be major sacrifices required of you.

I was terminated later that afternoon, via email, and barred from attending my students' graduation the following week. This absolutely crushed me. To add insult to injury, I had recently ruptured my Achilles tendon playing basketball and my wife was five months pregnant. So this put us in a tough spot regarding much-needed pay and health benefits.

Despite these very pressing realities, I was cut loose. I received no compassion from the people who should have been most compassionate. In that moment, my humanity meant nothing. My stellar job performance meant nothing. The strong relationships I built with my students and staff mates meant nothing. My life outside of work meant nothing. Presumably, I meant nothing. And this is a problem that so many teachers face: they are made to feel as if they mean nothing.

That they are nothing more than a clock-puncher or some number in an educational factory line. But this is not the truth! We are humans, and each of us means something to someone. This is why we need to stand up and speak out! This is why rebellion is necessary.

Should every single instructional minute matter, or should going outside for ten minutes to play every now and again matter more? Should nonstop academic engagement matter, or should social and emotional connections matter more? Should strictly following a pacing guide matter, or should being a teacher—being *that* teacher—matter more? We all know the answers, yet I wonder how many of us are willing to live them out. For the sake of our students and ourselves, we need to rebel!

"But What if I Get Fired?"

An objection I often hear in response to my encouragement to rebel is, "But my administrator will write me up, put me on some list, or worse, fire me. I can't lose my job! I just need to play the game on their terms." Listen, I hear you, and I can empathize with you in your concern. The possibility of losing one's job is a major deal, and I don't want anyone to feel as if I'm approaching this topic casually or from a place of indifference. The reality is that people have bills to pay; families need insurance; food has to be put on the table. So, losing a job, or even the chance of it happening, is no small thing.

> Losing a job is no small thing. But . . . losing yourself is no small thing, either.

But let's be clear: losing yourself is no small thing, either. Especially when you've worked hard to establish who you are as a person and a professional.

If, as a teacher, you find yourself being stripped of the joys of teaching, all because you must follow certain rules, *or else*, are you truly doing what you feel called to do? Under those guidelines, are you showing up daily as your most genuine self? Let's simplify things: *Are you happy?* For some, the answer might be yes. For many, it's no. For me, it's absolutely not! I could not live with myself if I chose not to be myself, to be human, first and foremost.

Humanity means that there *is* a possibility for you to fail, or in this case, be fired. That's life. But it also means that you have the right to live in freedom instead of fear. And if you allow the fear of someone or some system to rule over you, that bondage will crush you, and burn you out. Then, like many before you, you'll leave education altogether, most likely feeling ashamed or blaming yourself. Not because of the kids. Not because of teaching itself. But because fear robbed you of the things that make you happy. Because you heard, "Do as you're told, *or else*!" That's not right, y'all.

Of course, I want you to keep your job, but I also want you to keep your joy! Do what it takes to not get fired, but also do what it takes to keep your fire.

This is why I'm calling for balance. Adhere to the rules and norms that keep you safe and sane but push back against whatever threatens your peace. I am not suggesting that we rebel simply because we don't like something (or someone). I'm urging us to rebel against the things that harm us or push good teachers like us out of the classroom.

You deserve to be human, point-blank, period. To give breaks from work, to have fun, to go outside for a few lessons, to play games, to randomly watch a movie with your kids, to jump around through the pacing guide, to extend a lesson because it's been so amazing, to teach from the heart, and to be *that* teacher who creates joyful, memorable experiences in the classroom. You do not need permission to be free and to teach in a way that gives you life. Just do it.

Friends, I pray your teaching "ship" never goes down, but if it does, may it be because you rebelled and resisted in joy!

Opposition to Your Disposition

You're fired up and ready to rebel. Good! I can feel it coming from you! But being a rebel myself, I also know how quickly you'll be met with resistance. I know just how fast your friends, coworkers, or the leadership team can turn on you when you threaten to destroy their golden calf of normalcy. Change can be extremely difficult to make or accept, but changed dispositions are what change the system. When we think differently, we act differently. And when we rebel against what has been, this rebellion can positively impact what will be. Unfortunately, the powers that be, and those who love and have benefitted from the norm, won't let this happen easily.

As a rebel, you can be sure that you will face opposition to your fight. Someone is not going to like it when you question things or stand firm in saying no. Someone close to you will distance themselves from you to stop you from tearing down something that they hold near to their heart. Many people like the way things have always been or have grown comfortable and complacent with it, so naturally, they'll be resistant to any push for change. Yes, even change that could benefit them.

Instead of joining you in working to advance themselves or their situation, they'll work tirelessly to slow you down. They'll purposely get in your way. They'll do whatever they can to keep the status quo and to establish you as the bad guy. Instead of accepting your help or offering theirs, they'll attack your efforts; they might even attack your character. All because you chose to rebel. Here's what this opposition could sound like.

> The opposition: You think you're better than us, don't you?
> The rebel: No, I think we all deserve better, so I'm fighting for that.
>
> The opposition: Who do you think you are?
> The rebel: I know who I am. I'm *me*—qualified, competent, and compassionate. I'm standing firm in that.
>
> The opposition: You're too young and inexperienced.
> The rebel: I'm able to bring more to the table than you might think. Give me a chance to prove it.
>
> The opposition: You've been teaching for less than ten years. You don't know anything.
> The rebel: I don't have to be a veteran to try, to teach, and to serve well.

The opposition: I can tell you've got an agenda. Why else would you be fighting for this so hard?
The rebel: My only agenda is to love everybody and see to it that we all win.

The opposition: Nobody asked for your help.
The rebel: When there's a need or a gap, I step up to help fill it. That's just who I am.

The opposition: Just keep your head down and do your job!
The rebel: Fighting for myself and for others is my job.

The opposition: Ah, fresh out of college with bright eyes and big ideas. You'll become jaded like the rest of us soon enough.
The rebel: I choose how I respond to the things that happen around me.

The opposition: Why are you trying to mess up a good thing?
The rebel: Who is this good for? Who is it benefitting?

The opposition: We tried that years ago and it didn't work out.
The rebel: Thank you for sharing that. I believe it will work this time. Can we try it?

The opposition: You'll never change how things are done around here. Just stop trying.
The rebel: If I believed that, I wouldn't be here. I'm going to keep fighting!

The opposition: If you want things to be different, go somewhere else.
The rebel: No. I shouldn't have to leave just because people here don't want change. I'm staying, and I'm going to continue to bring about change.

Has anyone ever said anything like this to or about you? Have you caught the side-eye from administrators, parents, or even a previously trusted coworker? If so, they were in direct opposition to your disposition. They felt challenged by your longing for change or attacked by your intention to change what wasn't working. You wanted something better, while they had a mindset bent on preserving the norm. We must rebel against the norm—even if it's just us doing it!

Here's what we can do if we find ourselves entrenched in a battle like this:

- Seek out individuals whose views align with yours and who are like-minded in their desire to rebel against the norm. Social media can be excellent for this.
- Find a community outside of your school or workspace that can encourage you in the work you are doing and provide insights and information which can help you build at your school.
- Research people who are doing similar work and let them equip you with resources to continue your fight.

The Benefits of Rebelling

If you're able to push past the resistance, I think you'll find the benefits of your educational rebellion to be quite rewarding. Not only will your students be happier, but as a professional and a person, you will be filled with more joy. Fighting against what you believe to be wrong and making strides in that effort just makes you feel right! Two

> Fighting against what you believe to be wrong and making strides in that effort just makes you feel right!

major benefits of rebelling at school are less boredom and more time. Let's talk about them.

The Benefits of Less Boredom

Educational rebellion injects fun into the classroom. When an innovative teacher who is willing to read the room and bend the rules (when necessary) is in front of those kids, boredom has no place! The students will be engaged in what's happening and ever excited for what's next to come. Kids are used to the same ole, same ole, and become bored with that, so having someone who is willing to do things differently at the drop of a hat keeps them interested and engaged. It doesn't always have to be something big. It could be as simple as saying, "Yes, you all can use your cell phones for ten minutes," or "Let's close this up and take a walk around the school."

I had a sixth grader, B.J., once tell me, "Mr. Reed, I loved coming to your class on Monday mornings because we never knew what was gon' happen for the week." Did you catch that? A twelve-year-old from the West Side of Chicago told his former fifth grade teacher that he loved coming to school on Mondays! *Mondays*, people! "By the book" could never produce this! Rebels don't tolerate monotony. Rebels revolt against boredom. Rebels bring about the fun.

The Benefits of More Time

Another benefit of rebelling for teachers is caring for ourselves and reclaiming our time. There's an unwritten rule that teachers, and pretty much everyone else in society, ought to work our fingers down to the bone. Though bosses might not say it, it's expected that we stay after hours, take work home, and even work on the weekends. My Nana would say, "I rebuke that in the name of Jesus!" And I'm with you, Nana! Get ye that nonsense away from me!

Rebel against the suggestion, or the expectation, for teachers to do more. If you believe this in your heart, say the following with me:

I will not work after school if I don't want to.

I will rest over the evenings and the weekends.

I will use my PTO days whenever and however I feel I like it.

I will unashamedly spend time caring for myself and with my family and friends.

I will commit myself to rest.

This thinking is something I wish more educators would adopt. If you want to work more, that's your prerogative, and I make no judgments about your decision. But what we need to do as a community is rage against a system that clearly doesn't care about teachers—a system that doesn't care about people. About humans. We are the very reason school systems even continue to exist. So we must rebel against the notion that "more" is a must. That's a lie. That's the Man we need to fight. Fight the powers that be, and take back our time. This is a major benefit of rebelling.

Modeling Respectful Rebellion

We should also push back against what isn't working so that we can serve as a model for our scholars. Kids who see respectful, mindful adults questioning the status quo develop a greater understanding of their own power and capabilities. As it's been said, democracy is a verb. When we model these kinds of actions, our students will know what to do when they feel disempowered or when they feel like something isn't working for them.

I always let my scholars know, "I'm fine with you challenging something in a respectful way." In fact, few things bring me greater joy than when my students band together and say, "We put together a petition," or "We've decided that we don't agree with how you handled this. Can we discuss it?" I love that because I'm not insecure. I'm not bothered when my kids disagree with me because I know it's not necessarily an indictment against me. When they recognize they can question things and rebel, it makes them feel empowered to shake things up in their own world! This makes me so proud of them. So of course, I will continue to model respectful, educational rebellion in front of them. Be *that* teacher who rebels so that they can be *those* students who do the same.

A Brief Note to the Educational Rebel

Being an educational rebel can be a lonely and loveless journey. There will rarely be fanfare or flowers thrown at your feet because not many want to celebrate the individual responsible for being a disruptor. The people who choose not to see what you envision will make every day of your fight against a crooked system feel like a personal war with them, as if they've got beef with you because you're trying to do right by yourself or your kids. *It makes no sense.* But I'm here to tell you that you are not alone in this experience, nor are you the bad guy.

You are a light, and your fight should be celebrated. Remember what is at stake and the reason you chose to rebel against the norm in the first place. Be *that* teacher who is unafraid to fight for what's right. And keep laying the groundwork for those fighters and dreamers who will come after you. Persist! Onward! Rebel!

Reflections

Would you consider yourself a radical, a rebel, or a rule-follower in the school? Explain why you are one, two, or all three.

What norms exist at your school? In your classroom? Which norms need to be challenged, revised, or dropped? Why? Are the norms serving all populations as best they can? How can they be made more equitable?

_____

_____

What are you willing to rebel against, no matter who or what is on the other side?

_____

_____

Does every instructional minute matter to you the same way it does to some administrators, the state, or the school board? How can we make our classroom time most meaningful?

_____

_____

Burnout for teachers is real and is often prompted by difficult adults and overwhelming workloads. What things are you going to say yes or no to in order to keep yourself from burning out?

_____

_____

A Short Section on Saying No

Don't be afraid to tell your principal no. Yup. Straight like that.

Don't be afraid to tell your students no.

Do not be afraid to tell the parents and caregivers of your scholars no.

A well-placed no informs the recipient that you are a person who sets healthy boundaries for yourself. The intentional use of no reminds the hearer of your humanity and lets them know that you are not willing to budge or lose any piece of yourself just to appease them. You are a human being and have the right to say no with no explanation.

Amen?

Amen.

Rebel against the norm that suggests that teachers must agree to everything requested of them. You do not have to always say yes. Be reasonable and open to persuasion as appropriate, but do not fear standing firm with a no. You get to decide what you agree to.

One January, my principal asked me to run the program that helped kids memorize and perform Dr. Martin Luther King Jr.'s "I Have a Dream" speech. She said, "Mr. Reed, you're so talented and charismatic, so I just know you'll do an amazing job with our kids and make our school proud." She just *knew* I was going to say yes. I mean, it *is* Dr. King; and according to her, I *am* a dynamic speaker, I thought.

> You are a human being and have the right to say no with no explanation.

But then I remembered how busy I was and how much I just didn't want to do it, so I told my principal no. Was it scary? Sure. She was counting on me, and I was letting her and the entire school down, or so I thought. But sometimes, saying no to someone else means saying yes to yourself. We must be fine with that exchange. For our sake, we must become comfortable with saying no.

You do *not* have to stay after school past contracted hours, or come in hours earlier, or run a club, or run out for club sandwiches for a staff meeting, or meet with this group during your prep time, or prep five different groups for a performance during the all-school assembly, or assemble the Avengers! You are not Nick Fury!

As a result of saying no, you might fear retribution from your administrators. And you know what, I'm sorry that some school officials are petty and conduct themselves in this way. I've experienced a few administrators like this who power-trip and act like high schoolers with bruised egos. But know this, they're the ones who suck if their response to you setting boundaries is to punish you. That's on them and is an indication that it's time for you to consider if your current school is truly the place for you. There are plenty of great administrators elsewhere.

You might fear how your students will view you if you don't go along with their every wish. Maybe you won't be seen as the "cool teacher" anymore or the one who "gets" them and is just down to earth. Oh, well. That's life. They'll get over it and will be back to talking about sports, video games, or dance moves five seconds later.

Teachers, remember this: your supervisor is not the king, and your kids are not the boss. Yes, each has their own power and should get to control different dynamics of their workplace and school experience. But you have power, too! Other's desires do not negate your own, nor should they be considered more significant than yours. Both are equally important, and you ultimately have the right to decide how and when you want to move.

"No" is one of the most powerful words in your vocabulary. Protect yourself and protect your peace, beloved. Say no.

Reflections

As a teacher, what tasks, asks, or people do you find it difficult to say no to? What would your career look like if you were more eager to tell people no?

♪ Relationships mean
everything in school

Even more than academic
content and rules

Building them with kids
takes energy and work

But it all comes together when
you reach the heart first

It starts with an authentic
care and respect

Plus any other way
educators can connect

Reach 'em where they're at,
then keep it going after

And always remember,
the relationships matter.

CHAPTER 3
Relationships Matter

Our Words Matter

Kids don't hear the words they need often enough. Instead, they're told, "Do this!" or "Don't do that!" or "You should be here!" or "Why isn't this getting done?" Unfortunately, school can feel more like a prison than a safe place to learn and grow. And while some of our directives might be necessary, a command will never nourish a child's soul. A mandate will not build them up. Our kids don't always need to be told what to do. Rather, more often they need to be told who they are—someone's everything.

A huge part of my mission as an educator is to tell every one of my scholars that they mean something to this world and they mean something to me. Kids deserve to know that their teachers, as well as the other adults in their life, value and cherish them for just being themselves. For better or for worse, we can't control how our students are treated outside the classroom. But while they're in it, they should know their teachers care for them and think the world of them. That is something we can control.

One of the best ways to communicate this reality to students is through consistently explicit expression. In other words, say exactly how you feel about them and say it often! Think about a parent-child relationship or a marriage. In the sweetest relationships you know, the people involved frequently reiterate their care for each other. They regularly say things like, "You are special!" or "You mean the world to me!" Those words, said repeatedly, have significance.

As a teacher, when I utter similar words of care to my kids, naturally, they're expecting me to prove it. Kids know the deal: if you talk about it, you also have to be about it. Every statement commits you to following up by acting accordingly, or else it can be seen as fake. When you say it, display it. You must first audibly frame the way you feel about each scholar then prove it to them in tangible ways.

Think about how valuable a child would feel if you said, "Hey, it is so nice having you here in class today." Then you prove it by asking them to share their opinion on a topic that excites them. Yes, you're the one who has spoken, but they're the ones who feel heard! When you nourish them with your words, they'll be ready to run through a wall for you, or to at least turn in that assignment from yesterday.

> Think about how valuable a child would feel if you said, "Hey, it is so nice having you here in class today."

The research backs me up on the benefits of verbal affirmation for kids. Omar Gudiño, a clinical child psychologist and associate professor at the University of Kansas, asserts that affirmations from teachers boost a scholar's sense of self-confidence.[1] These kinds of affirmations can happen all the time, and they don't always have to be tied to schoolwork or academic accomplishments. Affirm your scholars about absolutely everything.

It was eighth-grade picture day—graduation photos—and one scholar, Corinne, questioned the outfit selection of another student,

---

1 Katie Loos, "Affirmations for Kids: How Parents Can Support Their Child's Learning," *U.S. News & World Report*, June 30, 2021, https://www.usnews.com/education/k12/articles/affirmations-for-kids-how-parents-can-support-their-childs-learning.

Kelis. It was almost as if Corinne was trying to belittle and bully her peer, but the thing was, Kelis was not going to be bullied!

On completing her up-and-down full-body scan of Kelis, Corinne asked, "Girl, *what* are you wearing?"

To that, Kelis, aware of the subtle jab being hurled her way, rolled her neck, raised her snapped fingers toward her side, then said, "*What I got on!*"

When I heard that, I couldn't help but cackle and become so filled with pride! Kelis was a student who often got picked on; but that day, she stood up for herself in a major way!

It was then that I loudly said, "*I know that's right*! You'd better represent and speak up for yourself." After saying that, two things happened: Corinne looked super salty, aware of her mistake, and didn't utter another word; and, more importantly, Kelis showcased the smallest but most satisfying smile. She knew she had been backed up and affirmed by her teacher. She was proud of herself and thankful for me! That's the power we have in verbally affirming our students.

I make it clear to my scholars that, no matter how our day goes, how I feel about them will never change. More importantly, what happens on any given day doesn't change how awesome they just are. I tell them, "I'm always gon' be your teacher, and y'all are always gon' be my kids! Even though y'all might get on my last nerve sometimes, I wouldn't trade you for the world." These words come every day, right before I release them outside for pickup after school.

Teachers, we should frequently say authentic and affirming words to our kids because they know, more than anyone else, that our words matter.

Their Words Matter

I once had a particularly impressive scholar named Kamry. Kamry was bright, a go-getter, full of energy, vocal, and a leader's leader. But sometimes children are not yet aware of the power they hold. Even if they are, they don't always use that power for good. Kamry was giving me such a hard time during class, and she made it known that she didn't like me at all. Wherever I was, she'd enter that space and sigh loudly enough so that everyone could hear it. Then, within earshot, she'd talk about me to her friends so I could hear her say over and over how she hated Mr. Reed (hey, at least she believes in consistently explicit expression).

Early in the school year, we were all at the annual Back to School Bash. Chicago juke music was blasting; kids were playing all sorts of games; the sugary drinks were flowing; and the scent of fresh hot dogs, hamburgers, and fries with mild sauce filled my nostrils. It was like Field Day, just at the beginning of school with a let's-have-a-great-year kinda vibe.

I saw Kamry standing by her big sister and sipping on Tampico punch. As usual, she didn't look too happy to see me, but honestly, I had a hunch that her hostility toward me wasn't about me at all. Never take it personally if you suspect a scholar might not like you. Though their dislike is aimed at you, it probably has nothing to do with you.

"Yo, yo!" I said to her with a smile. "I'ma keep it real with you—we just started the school year. Is there something I said to you that got you feelin' some type of way? Do my breath be stinkin' in class? What's good?"

"I just don't like you," she said bluntly. Straight like that. "I don't like you as my teacher."

"Okay," I responded with a smile. "I hear you. So you're not really feelin' me, but what about you? Tell me something about yourself!"

Remember, their words matter, too.

"Well, I'm a cheerleader. I travel with my squad all across the country to compete, and we be winnin'. I do other sports, too. And I'm in a bunch of after-school programs."

Standing there at the Back to School Bash, I learned about her hobbies and her heart. I then asked her about her thoughts on Hurricane Harvey, which had just ravaged parts of Texas. To my delight, she had some really cool ideas about how as a class we could help those who were suffering.

"Hey Kamry, I know you don't like me," I told her, "but I think you cool peoples." A slither of a smile made its way to the corner of her mouth. "Would you like to be in one of my classroom videos that I'll be posting to YouTube?"

"I guess, Mr. Reed," she replied.

I could tell that she wanted to be in it, especially since she had seen her friends in some of the other ones, but that she also didn't want me to know all that. *Ya'll know how kids be.* She played it cool, which was fine by me.

With her parents' permission, I recorded her telling me about her interests. She also reiterated her ideas of how we could help out the hurricane survivors.

I used Kamry's words in that moment to build a bond with her because, again, their words matter. That downtime at the Back to School Bash was really a come-up for both of us. To this day, we talk about her cheerleading and other extracurricular activities. Over the years, I've been to Kamry's band performances and basketball games, and I can't wait to attend her high school graduation! For a good chunk of that school year, she still pretended not to like me, but I could tell she was just fakin'. And at the end of the year, she even asked me if I'd take a picture with her to commemorate our great school experience together (her words, not mine). So, it came full circle. In August, I threw her in my school video, and by June, she practically begged me—the teacher she allegedly hated—to take a selfie with her. This is why relationships matter.

Opportunities Are Everywhere

There are opportunities everywhere for you to build relationships with your scholars. Before and after the school day come to mind as prime times to build strong connections with your kids. You could develop a special morning greeting with a student who gets dropped off early, then use it with them every single day. Or you could shoot hoops in the gym with some students before you make your morning copies or pouring that second cup of coffee. Quite often, I'll grab a few early bird scholars to help me with classroom setup in the morning. They help put down chairs, pass out papers, write things on the board, and sharpen pencils. Small stuff no doubt, but those small, collaborative moments provide big opportunities for us to chat. Truth be told, it's the smallest moments that often create the biggest impact. And as I've said before, clear and consistent dialogue means everything.

People will ask me, "How do you build these great relationships with your students?" My answer is always, talk with them! A simple, yet effective strategy to relationship-building is to make conversation with your scholars constantly. Those five-minute random chats add up quickly!

When I strike up a conversation with kids in those informal moments, such as during morning setup or while grabbing water after a game of HORSE, it's super organic. We're not talking about math, science, or history. We're usually talking about social media, sports, exciting plans for the weekend, an upcoming holiday, or their birthday. The good stuff! I figure we'll get to the academics during the rest of the day, but at that moment, it's our chance to talk about things that interest them. That's Relationship Building 101. Please don't miss this.

Dr. Daniela O'Neill, professor of developmental psychology at the University of Waterloo, has demonstrated through her research that small talk between adults and kids is actually a huge win for the kids! In a speech she gave, she mentions a study that found that the amount of words addressed to a child correlates with the child's vocabulary years later.[2] Small talk adds up, so even if casual chats with your kids aren't really your thing, try your best to make them your thing!

---

2 "Dr. Daniela O'Neill - Small Talk with Big Outcomes for Children," Urban Child Institute, March 20, 2015, http://www.urbanchildinstitute.org/resources/videos/dr-daniela-oneill-small-talk-with-big-outcomes-for-children.

The period just after school ends offers ample time to bond with your students, too. Sometimes, parents and caregivers take a while to pick up their kids, or the older kids just like to linger around their safe space known as school. This can be fine because it gives you an opportunity to chop it up with that one scholar who's left waiting or who chooses to stick around just cause. There's always one. My advice is to use that time as an investment. Don't waste those precious moments by just standing there awkwardly and silently. Talk! Ask questions and follow up with your input. Laugh and learn! Those ten free minutes with Johnny or La'Keisha will pay dividends when you have a block period or an entire day with them tomorrow.

The same approach applies when I pass by a current or former student of mine in the hallway. They appreciate that I acknowledge their existence by speaking to them. It makes them feel remembered. Seen. Loved. I ask, "What's up?" and even develop little inside jokes with some of them. That's our thing and it remains our thing whenever we see each other. It's an ongoing conversation, forever. Talk!

Eat with Your Students

Never underestimate the connection involved with breaking bread with someone. As teachers, we're missing out if we aren't taking advantage of this time to develop relationships with our students. Meals make us feel safe. Being able to share a meal with someone allows us to be more vulnerable, open, and honest. It might sound weird, but whenever I eat with my scholars for the first time, they're surprised because they don't expect me to be someone who eats some of the same foods as they do. It's bizarre to them, and hilarious to me.

They ask, Mr. Reed, what you know about them Cool Ranch Doritos?

"Man, I been eatin' these since before you was born, lil homie!" I say.

Or I'll hit them with the, "So, y'all just gon' eat Honey Buns and candy for lunch today, huh? Where's all the fruit and salad at?"

A lot of kids won't get to experience this friendly jabbing with adults if their teachers don't eat with them from time to time. Now, I'm not saying give up your entire lunch or prep. I'm saying, pop into the cafeteria for two minutes, ask a question, tell a joke, share a smile, then be about your business. A lunch-time interaction with students in the cafeteria might not curb someone's hunger, but it can feed someone's soul. Be *that* teacher.

> A lunch-time interaction with students in the cafeteria might not curb someone's hunger, but it can feed someone's soul.

I've found that kids love it when teachers pull them out for the occasional meal away from the cafeteria, too. Some teachers call this a lunch bunch. They grab a few kids and just eat lunch with them in the classroom. Deep relationships can be built while sharing a meal because that time lends itself to sharing your heart. It's hard to continue to feel salty about negative behavior from earlier or for them to hold a grudge against you for something you did, when everyone's chomping on some chips or someone has peanut butter stuck to the roof of their mouth. Sharing a meal humanizes everyone involved—that's what education is about. You'll share stories about family meals, cultural dishes, funny experiences, and your own past. Don't be a stranger to your scholars. Let food bring y'all together.

By the way, if a kid gives you some of their Flamin' Hot Cheetos or Takis, you know they *truly* love you. You've made it into their good graces; kids are not quick to part ways with those hot chips!

Connecting throughout the Day

So, we talk, we eat, and now we move on to some fun! Visiting scholars during recess or gym class is another opportunity to build relationships. Get movin' and be a part of wherever there's movement going on. Playing games with students builds trust and shows them you can be fun, too. I toss touchdown passes all day to my kids playing football, and am quick to spike a volleyball that's been set to me perfectly by one of my students! Yeah, I'm *that* teacher!

William Massey, an assistant professor at Oregon State University, conducted research into the benefits of teacher-student play. The results were golden, as expected. He says, "Recess can also be an opportunity for teachers and students to interact in more informal settings, for teachers to model healthy behavior and appropriate social skills and for students and teachers to develop stronger relationships. Importantly, other research has shown these factors contribute to student success."[3]

One year, my students didn't have a lot of equipment to use during recess, which I thought was unfair. So, I went out and bought some jump ropes for them. I happened to know that one of my girls, Yanni, jumped Double Dutch competitively, so I wanted to give them supplies to practice with at school. When I finally gave Yanni and her friends the jump ropes, they thanked me and shooed me away.

Kids.

"Don't get it twisted, though," I said to them. "Y'all know I used to do Double Dutch for real, right?"

Of course, they laughed at me, but I promised them that one day I'd show them how Mr. Reed used to get down.

During Double Dutch, two ropes are rotating at the same time but in opposite directions, so the challenge is to jump in-between the ropes safely without getting smacked in the face. Yeah, it gets real.

---

3   Michelle Klampe, "Study Finds Adults Play a Key Role in Recess Participation," *Synergies*, August 23, 2018, https://synergies.oregonstate.edu/2018/adults-key-role-recess-participation/.

One recess, I took off my jacket and school lanyard and told the young ladies who were playing I was going to jump in. More kids gathered around and watched me. Maybe they hoped I'd succeed, or maybe they hoped I'd get popped in the face.

"In, in, in, in!" the girls chanted as I navigated the ropes.

One of the rope-turners was not doing a good job, and I got hit in the face.

Guess that was payback for something.

But after that small hiccup, I jumped in successfully and showed everyone my skills.

I will never forget what happened next. Those kids could not stop talking about my performance. I bet they'll always remember the moment their teacher literally jumped into their lives.

Be *that* teacher who's not afraid to get their hands dirty. Be *that* teacher who's willing to get on their level, be it outside, at PE, or in the lunchroom, because they deserve someone who will meet them exactly where they're at with love. Those are the kinds of relationships that matter. A word of advice, though: keep a little extra deodorant stored in your desk and you'll be all good.

Connection through Communication

The short of it is this: we always have to be ready to connect. Most often, that connection comes through communication. If the school day is a book, then class time is the text. In between the lines of that text is your chance to listen to your students and develop a dialogue with them. A relationship with our scholars is an ongoing conversation, and every day is a chance to tell a kid something that may very well change their life. In fact, a child might remember something you say today for the rest of their life! So, choose your words wisely, and use those words often.

As educators, when you take advantage of those "random" moments of chatting, you'll start to build a steady rapport with your students that isn't random at all. Before you know it, you'll know the kids very well, and they'll know you. Then they'll be more inclined to hear about all the cool stuff you know and are willing to teach them!

Look for chances to make conversation while you're not in your normal role at the head of the classroom. I recommend you dribble a few basketballs with your students, race them from the playground to the door of the classroom, and pop into their music class to sing a few notes with them. These moments give your scholars a chance to see you as a human. Teaching is about rehumanizing the educational experience for everyone. Use every minute away from schoolwork to put in the work of building relationships with them. In education, relationships matter most.

> A child might remember something you say today for the rest of their life! So, choose your words wisely and use those words often.

Reflections

What is something good you remember a teacher, peer, or another person saying to you or about you that has always stuck with you? How did it make you feel? Is there something similar you can say about any of your scholars today?

_____

_____

_____

_____

What kinds of things can you say to make sure your students know how you feel about them? What can you say about them to help them know they belong in your classroom? Do you think they just know? How can they? We must tell them.

_____

_____

_____

_____

Not every student we encounter will be our favorite (and vice versa). Nonetheless, everyone deserves to be respected and treated with dignity. When a kid is not your cup of tea, how can you ensure that your biases have been placed aside? Think about ways you can grow to appreciate those scholars overtime.

Where do you struggle in the relationship-building process? Where are you successful?

_____

_____

_____

_____

Where can you develop out-of-class rapport with your students—lunch, recess, gym, hallways, after school pickup, technology, home-economics, choir, etc.? Consider the places where you can connect outside of the academic space of your classroom.

_____

_____

_____

_____

*Something that I wonder, is
it all about the numbers?*

*Or does who a student is at
their core matter, too?*

*Of course, it's the latter, everything
ain't 'bout the data*

*Those things can't tell the
story like relationships do!*

CHAPTER 4

Gather the Real Data

Everything has seemingly become about numbers, letters, grades, and scores. In other words, data, data, data. Maybe the saddest part is that the increase in testing doesn't even correlate with improvements in students' ability to learn happily or think critically. On the contrary, it's been found that more testing only serves to raise children's anxiety![1]

Here's my suggestion: In addition to following their academic progress, how about we collect data on who our students are as people? Their interests and hobbies. How they feel about their culture. What life is like at home or away from school. What they think about the climate of your classroom or the culture of your school. Any of the things they feel comfortable sharing with us.

This would tell us far more than how they perform on some random test. Sure, we need to know where they are academically so that we can know where to help them, but our kids are more than a score. They're more than how they perform on a test the one day they take it. They are their passions, their relationships, their aspirations, and their dreams over time. They are who they've been their entire lives. And more importantly, they are becoming who they will be moving forward.

---

1 King, H., (n.d.), *Standardized Testing Proves to Be Ineffective and Overwhelming for Students*, The Wingspan. Retrieved April 17, 2022, from https://www.cfwingspan.com/2216/opinion/standardized-testing-proves-to-be-ineffective-and-overwhelming-for-students/.

When we use the data that we gather about our kids as people to fuel the relationships we have with them, we will be able to better serve them. It is my core belief that information is a pathway to empathy. This means the more about someone we know, the more grace and compassion we'll be able to show.

Instead of teaching to a test, we should let our kids teach us about themselves. The what, why, and how of education should be informed by who our scholars are and by everything they're willing to tell us.

The Data That Matters

I like to call the information I learn about my kids relational data. Everything a student tells me about themselves or that I pick up along the way goes into a mental relationship database I keep on them. That's the data in my brain.

But not all information gets filed in the same way or in the same place for every student. Teachers must work at finding out how to use the specific feedback each kid gives them in a way that suits that particular child. As data-analyzing experts, educators understand that what works well academically for one student might not always work well for another. The same is true for the relational data we collect.

For example, Shakira might tell me that she's into fishing, nature, and spending time outdoors with her grandpop. Of course, I'll try to play with those pieces of information as long as I can, working bits about nature into all sorts of class activities for her. I might also take my students outside on a sunny day with Shakira in mind, knowing she thrives outdoors. That's intentional teaching. That's the benefit of using the data I've discovered about that child.

On the other hand, Quincy doesn't care a lick about fish and trees! He's made it clear that his favorite place to be is inside, under the AC, on his phone, talking or playing games with his homies.

"Outside be too hot, Mr. Reed," he says.

And look, Q, I agree.

Since I know Quincy is extremely vocal, personable, and more of a social butterfly, I'll give him roles and responsibilities on group assignments (inside the school building) that I'm confident he'll excel at and lead others in. Again, this is me playing to the strengths I've learned he has.

As a teacher, it's not all about what I give my students. I must appropriately manage what a kid chooses to give me, fighting to see every bit of information as valuable and usable for the purposes of teaching and serving *that child*. This is teaching with intentionality.

It's my responsibility to figure out how to work the relational data—how to make the best use of what the data is telling me. The stuff that interests your students should be the stuff that you work hard to find interesting for yourself.

Why not attempt to engage our scholars with the things we know engage them already? Erika Patall, assistant professor in the Department of Educational Psychology at the College of Education at The University of Texas, confirmed through her research that student interest is a strong predictor of the student's level of engagement both with the classroom material and with the teacher. Patall says, "Interest was a powerful predictor of students' effort, participation, attention, and thinking in the classroom, especially for underrepresented minority students who reported thinking more about how to learn in science class on days they experienced interest during that class."[2]

Full transparency, I let my scholars drive my instruction. Sure, I have a plan set in place as far as what I'm going to teach each day, but I ultimately base everything on their unique questions and musings. If they ask something that gets us going left, we're going left a little while. If a student poses a statement that moves us right, we're gonna go right for a little bit.

---

[2] *New Research Indicates Student Interest Critical to Engagement in Science*, College of Education, University of Texas at Austin, July 20, 2020, retrieved April 17, 2022, from https://education.utexas.edu/news/2016/08/10/new-research-indicates-student-interest-critical-engagement-science.

Children should be in charge of their learning. What's important is not just what we adults want to teach. What and how kids want to learn is also essential.

What Is the Data Showing Me?

Ask yourself this question: What is the data showing me? What are my kids telling me they like or care about? What clues are they constantly dropping that I need to pick up on and work with? What is the stuff that's going to motivate them to learn more or keep them curious and inquisitive in my classroom? What things make them believe learning is truly fun?

I'll tell you one thing, it ain't long passages taken from stories they would never read on their own, or confusingly worded questions from a boring test.

That stuff doesn't matter to our kids. And why should it?

The things that matter to our students are the things they tell us matter to them. Once we finally listen to what they've been communicating all along, then everything begins to click! That's where the magic happens! That information becomes our map, our GPS, and our Bible for that scholar. When we see what the data shows us, we must go where the data's itching to take us!

Applying the Data

Here's what I think data should stand for: Data should Always Turn into Application! The treasured information we learn about our students should be used to fuel the relationships we have with them. One easy way to go with the data is by making a big deal about the things you notice your scholars making a big deal about.

Personally, I don't care about video games or some of the viral dances that are all the craze (probably because I can't dance). But if my kids are into that stuff—which they are—you'd better believe that I'm going to make references to those things during instruction. I'll even try busting a move during class, though it'll probably make me look cringe. Just the fact that I merely know about the things they care about means something to them. It's relational currency they will always be willing to accept. Nobody's turning down that relational data dollar!

Many educators frequently talk about "buy-in" and getting our scholars to invest themselves into the content we're "selling." But what if we switched that model up? What if teachers were the ones to make the relational investment into what our kids were selling? If we deposit our interest, our energy, and our efforts into their relationship bank, that effort will always pay back dividends!

My social media friend and teacher extraordinaire, Michael Bonner, puts it this way: "You can't demand a withdrawal from someone you've never invested in." This is to say, if you're not showing an interest in what they're giving you, you can't possibly expect them to give you much else. Teachers, you don't have to like the video games, the dances, etc., but at least show your students you're listening when they talk about those things.

When a child keeps saying, "Look at what I can do," and the adults around them pay no mind, eventually they'll stop asking you to look. They'll stop caring. They'll become apathetic. May this never be the case in our classrooms! Be *that* teacher who looks, listens, and learns everything they can about their students, then applies actions based on the data they see.

One time, I was talking in the hallway with one of my scholars who had just gotten her hair done, dyed, and loc'd up.

"I like your hair," I said to Bailey. "What's that style called?"

"They called fox locs, Mr. Reed," she said, as she playfully rolled her eyes at me.

I scrunched my face a bit. "Oh, cause they got all that red in it, right? Like a fox?"

"No, they just called fox locs cause that's what they call them!"

"F-O-X?" I skeptically spelled out to her.

"No, it's F-A-U-X. *Fox*!"

I replied, "I think you mean to say, '*foh*,' Bailey."

She hit me back with the, "I think you don't know how to spell, Mr. Reed."

Well, we agreed to disagree, but I could tell that Bailey had fun teaching me a little something about her unique hairstyle. I took an interest in the thing that really interested her, and the "fox locs" joke was one of our personal connections for the rest of the school year. I even told her that I wrote about this interaction we had, and she blushed red, just like a fox, knowing I included her and her cool hair in my story. That's the specific data that matters.

Keep Askin' Questions—Ask to Act!

So, now you understand why gathering relational data is important, but how should you gather it? Easy. Ask your scholars questions. I am always, *always* asking questions. Even if I don't get answers at that moment, that's okay. What I'm making clear to my students, behind every inquiry, is that they will forever have someone who wants to get to know them and cares about them in that way.

And I don't just ask questions at the beginning of the year or when a new student arrives. I want to get to know my kids the entire time I'm in front of them, day one to day 185. Even when they're away from me. That's the way a solid relationship should work. While you can never fully know someone, learning about them and learning to appreciate who they are can be exceptionally fun.

I don't just come with stock questions. Sure, I might use a few as a baseline, but after that, it's an open field. My next question is fueled by their last answer. I'm on a bus that my kids are driving, so buckle up! And to be real, I'm just happy to be along for the ride.

"My lil baby cousin lives with us," one will say.

"Oh, word? What's his name? How old is he?" I'll ask.

And then that student will complain that his three-year-old cousin, Man-Man, is annoying and is constantly singing some super kiddie song.

"Ah. So do you not like that song?" I'll ask. "Because me and my daughter think it's a bop! What kind of music do you listen to?" I'll follow up with.

What I'm doing is literally going off what they give me and taking the dialogue in new and unpredictable directions, which again, can be so fun. Notice that I'm always directing the conversation toward learning about who they are. The more they give me, the more I take and invest back into the conversation and the relationship with them later on. It's a process that all starts with asking questions.

It's my belief that no teacher has an excuse for not gathering personal data from their students. If you've got time to ask your students where their pencil is or why they haven't finished an assignment, you've got just as much time to ask if they did anything cool over the weekend and follow up with more discussion.

We have a choice for how to spend those precious moments we're given. If we choose to invest the time and energy on the front end, we will be blessed with better rapport and engagement on the back end of things. Don't get me wrong, intentionality takes time; but over time, you'll always be blessed with more quality time. Intentionality with your students creates more time for fun, more space to create good memories, and ultimately more justification to have those much-needed heart-to-heart, come-to-Jesus conversations.

> If you've got time to ask your students where their pencil is... you've got just as much time to ask if they did anything cool over the weekend.

Ask questions, then do something with the information they give you. Don't just ask to ask—ask to act!

Try using student interest inventories and surveys where they tell you the basic—but important!—things about themselves. Ask about family, pets, favorite foods, favorite places to go, and dream jobs. And that's just the low-hanging fruit! You can always go more in depth, but this is a solid place to start. And hey, use the information they give you. Don't have them write or talk about things just to let those things fall on the floor. Grab what gets thrown out there and find a way to use it. Be *that* teacher.

How to Use Relational Data

About a month into each new school year, I'll write two questions on the whiteboard: What do you think about yourself? and What do you think Mr. Reed thinks about you?

I'll then give each scholar the opportunity to ponder my questions. Later, they share their responses with me privately through writing or conversation, if they're up for that.

Some of the comments are hilarious, and others can be quite gutting. Either way, their answers immediately impact the way I interact with them.

In response to one of those questions one year, Josh wrote, "Mr. Reed thinks I'm smart and funny, but prolly that I be a lil irritating cause I talk a lot."

As the true teacher that I am, I gave Josh some written feedback. I wrote, "Look, you said it, not me." With a smiley face next to it. A little jokey joke for levity.

But it didn't stop there. *Because* he was so talkative, or brilliantly expressive, rather, I wanted to use that quality for good. Every week from that point on, I gave Josh two or three minutes on Monday mornings to be a talk show host. He had become our class's very own Chicago news reporter, and he'd eagerly fill us in on current events that took place over the weekend—some local, others national or global. That was his way to shine!

We took what could have been a negative and turned it into a positive. But don't miss this—I wouldn't have been able to do that if I never posed that initial question. Don't just read the data, do something with it.

What negatives can you choose to see in a positive light? How can you intentionally transition your thinking away from a deficit mindset regarding your students and into asset-based thinking? We can't always get what we want, so we must be down to work with what we've got. Dig deep, mine for content by asking questions, then brush off the dirt once you find those data diamonds.

Start the Year with Scholars, Not Scores

One year, all the kids were taking their beginning-of-the-year standardized tests. A coworker had noticed that a scholar I used to teach was rushing through the test. She also saw on his face that the boy had become frustrated. The teacher contacted me because she knew that I had developed a decent relationship with this particular kid. She wanted me to give him a brief pep talk, which I gladly agreed to do. After I did exactly that, my colleague let me know that the kid had slowed down and actually ended up being one of the last to finish his test that day. Better still, he ended up exceeding the mark he had anticipated hitting on the exam.

Data should be about the scholar, not the score.

One of my students, Sydney, was scribbling on a Post-it Note before this very test. She wrote to herself, *Yo, you got this, SD! Can't nobody do SD like SD do SD.* Confusing to me, but I guess it made total sense to her.

I looked over her shoulder, and while I thought I knew what the note meant, I had to ask.

"Sydney, who's SD?"

> Data should be about the scholar, not the score.

"That's me, Mr. Reed! C'mon now."

I laughed. "Ah, okay! I love the self-motivation. You do you, SD!"

I needed her to know that I appreciated the fact that she pushed herself and psyched herself up. From that point on, I would refer to Sydney as SD.

A few months later, I asked her if anyone else called her by that name.

"Nah, you the only one, Mr. Reed. And I'm cool with that."

We exchanged smiles.

The test she took gave me data about math, science, language arts, and reading. The interaction we had before the test gave me data about her as a person. Years later, Sydney and I remember the latter. That's the data that matters.

The truth is that there's no such thing as a standardized child. So in my opinion, it doesn't make sense to focus solely on standardized tests. Are we trying to train kids to be cookie-cutter models, or should we be trying to push them to be the best version of themselves? The latter only works when we get to know who they are, not when we train them to do well on a test. They're not dogs or robots or artificial intelligence.

Be *that* teacher who learns who every individual student is and serves and loves them in a way that suits *them*. Data from tests can be useful, but it can never reveal the whole story. Relational data about *who our scholars are* can revolutionize teaching and education for the better. You've gotta believe me on this one. I've got the data to back it up. The stuff that truly matters is the stuff that matters to them.

Reflections

Which means more to you and why: academic data or relational data? What does this mean in your classroom or in terms of building relationships with kids? Are the relationships lacking? If not, are there areas where the academics are lacking? How can you grow to be more well-rounded with all the data you collect and apply?

_____

_____

_____

_____

We don't all share the same interests, especially with kids. But, in what ways can you deepen your interests into the things your kids like? Commit to trying something that they like just once and see what happens!

It can be tempting to deliver one-size-fits-all educational experiences: free time, phones for ten minutes, extra recess. Those are quick and easy, and seemingly rewarding for everyone, but this is not always the case. What can you do to differentiate the relationship-building opportunities and experiences students get to have in your classroom?

_____

_____

_____

_____

What are the potential benefits of you investing time and energy into truly getting to know your students? The personal benefits? Professional? Academic? Classroom culture and climate? Are there any drawbacks?

___

___

___

I have said to my students, "The more we know, the faster we'll grow and the further we'll go." What do you think about this quote? Does this quote ring true for you when gathering relational data about your students?

___

___

___

*How do you see me?
Can I just be me?*

*Or is me an offense to
your white picket fence?*

*It wouldn't make sense if
you didn't see the real me*

*The human, the beauty,
the life—ya feel me?*

CHAPTER 5

How Do You See Me?

Of all the chapters in this book, this is the one I thought about and worked on the most. I feel such a responsibility to get it right and to empower you to go into your classrooms, schools, and communities and be the antiracist champion we need right now. But I'm also conscious of how I'm not in your shoes and that there are many ways to be in this world. Still, I couldn't write about education without addressing how racism impacts our students and without sharing tools I've seen be effective at serving our students through a racial lens, both inside and outside the classroom.

For me, any discussion of racism in education comes under the broader mandate I have—to rehumanize the classroom and, by extension, our communities. Being antiracist must begin with the fundamental belief that every human is equally valuable. In the Bible, this concept comes from what's known as the *imago Dei*, which states that each of us is made in the image of God. In His sight, we are all equally valuable. But it's important to understand that believing in this doctrine, whether Christian or not, is not enough to be an antiracist teacher. As with all things, genuine belief must compel genuine action.

Rehumanizing education means not just believing in the inherent value of every student but also acting on that belief. It means coming to understand something about someone, then doing something with that knowledge. This understanding encompasses all kinds of things, like race, immigration status, and neurodiversity. I'm focusing on race in this chapter, particularly interactions with Black students, because it is something I am well positioned to speak about as a Black man who is an educator and was once a Black child in the public school system. My hope is that you take the tenets from this chapter and apply them to other identities of the children in your classroom. I will leave the discussion of those matters to others who specialize in them.

But in this chapter, buckle up cause we finna talk about race.

What's Race Got to Do with It?

So, what does it mean to rehumanize the educational experience through the context of race? It means educators must think about the humans in front of them through a racial lens. Race, though it is a social construct, brings about certain realities that we must take seriously and handle delicately. For example, many in our society see those beautiful and brilliant Black children as a threat. You, however, must see those beautiful and brilliant Black children as a promise! Note though, that in both cases, the race of the child is seen. Don't fool yourself by pretending that race isn't a significant factor in our schools. It is.

There is absolutely no space in our communities for so-called color-blindness or any well-meaning but tremendously harmful sentiments such as, "I don't see color." *Yes*, you do. Our schools do. Those soul-crushing suspension rooms, expulsion committees, and alternative programs do. The minds of racist educators do. So, the quicker you can acknowledge that race impacts your classroom (whether you have Black students or not) and work with what you see, the better those brilliant and beautiful Black kids (and everyone else's brilliant and beautiful kids) will be! Rehumanizing education through the context of race means seeing each child as they are, then treating them with the respect and dignity they deserve.

Be Intentional about Seeing Them

The process of seeing students, particularly Black students, as they are doesn't just happen on accident or by chance. It happens by choice. Considering the realities each child faces then serving them accordingly comes down to intentionality. It's not some multiple choice test where you don't have to study and can just guess and hope for the best. No, this kind of work is like an essay that requires you to put forth substantial thought and effort. There must be a game plan before you write, revisions as you work, and an expectation that your words and actions will impact others. We're dealing with the learning and the lives of children who want to be something and deserve to become that. If you don't see that and see them in this way, you are in their way.

Or maybe you've got no problem with intentionality, but you just feel like kindheartedness or love should get the job done. To this I say, yes, lead with love—but then what? What's love got to do with it if not followed up by action? Is that really even love? I don't think so. If you want to be an antiracist educator, you must find or make your own model to engage purposefully with the Black, brown, or other minority students you're called to serve. You must educate yourself and properly inform your white students, too. You must discover what your role in this work is, then live up to your responsibility. Step one is seeing someone as they are, and not just for those who have physical eyesight. Human beings truly seeing and valuing people as they are takes work. Hard work. Heart work! But you can do this work!

There are many more qualified and scholarly folks who can give you a template for how to do some of this work, but the work will have to be individual to you. Other people are not at your school, you are. I am not with your students, you are. This individual work could involve looking into your own implicit biases or challenging your own preconceived ideas about certain kids. Or even better, questioning your school's policies which inadvertently or intentionally disadvantage students of color.

The essential questions worth your consideration are as follows: What efforts must I make to see and treat the people around me, no matter their skin color, as human? What must I do to see the people in front of me as they are? How can I best treat children as humans, equal to me? These questions and their answers should remain front of mind.

My Experiences and Perspectives on Race in Schools

When I am presenting to teachers and other school officials, I'm often asked about my own experiences as a Black child in the public school system and how that has informed my career as an educator. I'll share those experiences with the caveat that they're individualized, subjective experiences. I hope you can extract some meaning and insight from them. I will also ask you to reflect on questions I've carefully placed throughout this chapter. Then I'll get into a few best practices I've seen and underline what I said above—this is not a blueprint. This is a map of where some people have been.

How They Saw Me

My experiences as a Black child were free of the overt racism they make Hollywood movies about. No one called me the N-word. No school official threw me on the ground in a hallway after suspecting me of a crime or disrespect (although, unfortunately, too many of our Black and brown children are subjected to this every day). But there is no getting away from the fact that Black scholars, as a whole, are under surveillance in schools in ways that white students are not.

You'll recall the example I used earlier of the fourth-grade teacher who sent me to the principal's office because she thought I was trying to be disruptive, even though I wasn't. Mrs. Jansen was white, and I have no doubt that she considered me a threat even when my motives were innocent due to her unconscious bias. For example, she was always really nice to Andy, one of the white children in class. To her, Andy, a white boy, could do no wrong. Now, this ain't no shade to Andy or any of the other white kids in my fourth-grade class. They were actually super cool. But it definitely gave the rest of us Black kids a hint as to who was good by our teacher's standards and who was not. We could just tell how Mrs. Jansen saw Andy versus how she saw us.

At this same school, we had a program that spotlighted a different kid each week. Sorta like a weekly MVP award for kids. One student in each class would be selected to receive the honor and represent their classroom. Over the course of a year, the prize rolled around in no particular order—each kid won it two or three times. Although the order was supposedly random, I was selected last every time. It couldn't have been alphabetical because my last name was not at the end of the alphabet. It wasn't based on height or in some other arbitrary feature. And still I was last. Maybe she just didn't like me. That's certainly possible. But at nine years old, this reality told me everything I needed to know about how my teacher viewed me: least deserving of any honor. *And as a child*, I thought it was because I was Black.

These things happen all the time in our schools. Kids are absorbing and making meaning of the small moments in which their educators truly show their colors. But the small moments aren't really small at all; they are significant, and inevitably have a major impact. The experience of either being overwhelmingly surveilled or severely overlooked mars the way our kids come to understand how or where they fit in the world. How we see our students often shapes how they see themselves.

> **The small moments aren't really small at all.**

Although the weekly honor experience impacted how I view certain teachers, I'm not recalling it to rehash my trauma. I'm using it to illustrate how important it is to be mindful of how you look at your students. There must be a certain intentionality to see past your initial thoughts. The first way of seeing your scholars isn't always the best way, so a re-envisioning process is almost always necessary.

It's easy to tell ourselves that at first glance so-and-so is a troublemaker or can't sit still or doesn't listen or probably won't meet their academic goals. But just because it's easy to think those things doesn't make it right. We must challenge ourselves to detect patterns in those gut reactions, disrupt them, and dismantle the systems of thinking that generate them.

Here's a question I'd like you to consider: What biases might students *think* you hold about them and why (e.g., boys vs. girls, quiet learner vs. more expressive, well-behaved vs. more in need of support, Black vs. white, etc.)? How can you upend these biases and confirm to your students that they're being treated equitably?

The extension of what happened between me and Mrs. Jansen in the fourth grade is that it seeped into my fifth-grade year, too. I had my first Black teacher when I was ten years old, so double-digit Dwayne was ready to turn up! But Ms. Carter was not a fan of young Mr. Reed either, and I could tell. The part that trips me up the most is that I overheard my fourth-grade teacher dropping a bug in Ms. Carter's ear that I was one to "look out for." Ms. Carter ate that right up. From the jump, I was the little Black boy who was trouble, or so I was made to believe. Many years later, I realized a valuable lesson—white supremacy can infect anyone, racism can be internalized, and kids can be put in no-win situations before they've even lost their baby face. Let's just say I had been a troublemaker in fourth grade—which I wasn't—I still should have been given the grace and leeway to do better the following year. But my reputation had already preceded me and practically sealed the deal by the time I got to Ms. Carter. How one teacher saw me became how the next teacher saw me, and I had no chance at redemption. I hate it.

Thank God I didn't internalize this thinking and begin to seek out trouble. Unfortunately, that's the pathway for many students who experience this sort of labeling.

My fifth-grade teacher was fundamentally put off by me, and I think it all started with how my fourth-grade teacher saw and labeled me. This was a shame because, by that time, I really could have used a strong Black role model in the classroom. But what I came to understand is that just because you're Black (or any other minority or marginalized population) that doesn't mean you automatically become a good role model to those you serve. You must play your role and model it well to be considered a good role model. I share this anecdote to illustrate that while representation is critical, it also isn't the whole answer.

> You must play your role and model it well to be considered a good role model.

How Do You See Schools with Black and Brown Kids?

Moving from my experiences as a student to my observations as a teacher, one small thing I want to encourage you to do to create antiracist spaces is to analyze your school and classroom policies. As we discussed earlier, many times school rules are born out of racism and discrimination. The argument for these rules is usually in the interest of safety or because it's the way things have always been done. But many common procedures in schools were instituted to insulate and protect whiteness, while simultaneously attacking and policing students of color.

Think about the zero-tolerance policies, which were rampant in many schools (especially charter schools with large minority racial groups) throughout the early 2000s. Or what about movements to cut Black hair, like dreadlocks, that have taken place more recently. I have never heard about a white student having to shave their hair off before being granted access to walk across a graduation stage. But I have for Black kids.

Hair and headwear have been big issues in schools for a long time. Not just anyone's, though. Particularly Black hair and head coverings. Consider the school dress codes that set their aim on hats and hoods, among other things. Based on my experiences in schools, these policies, among others, have targeted Black and brown students and are fundamentally grounded in keeping those children of color "in their place." Anything to strip students of color of their dignity or right to expression seems acceptable at many schools. The justifications given for the enforcement of these rules are about safety, engagement, and uniformity, but they just don't make any sense.

And I know one objection will be, "But these headwear policies exist in schools with majority white populations, too!" True as that might be, that doesn't mean that the rule, in its essence, isn't intended to go after Black and brown students, or that it isn't in place to create a culture that spreads in hopes of catching the Black and brown kids who disobey. Or that it isn't already set in stone in case students of color happen to transfer into the all-white school community. For reference, there are white people incarcerated in American prisons across the nation for drug distribution, but that doesn't mean the laws weren't set up to specifically target people of color.[1]

Rarely would there be an issue if Scott, a white student, came to school one day with a baseball cap, or Jenny, another white student, donned a golf visor during a bad hair day. But let Malik rock his snapback cap or Daisha sport her bandana, then it's "Take that off" or "Go to the office." Why is that? It's often an issue of discrimination. When school rules don't apply to everyone, or when administrators

---

1 Michelle Alexander, *The New Jim Crow: Mass Incarceration in the Age of Colorblindness* (New York: New Press, 2012).

and teachers pick and choose when to enforce certain rules, their biases come into play, and they are discriminating against specific people—against specific kids! *What are we doing?*

This is dehumanizing and completely unacceptable.

I'm speaking extensively about the hair and headwear thing because it's a big deal. People of color have a unique relationship with our hair. Often, it is a huge part of our identity. Of our humanity. That's why if the hairdresser or someone's auntie can't finish our braids over the weekend, or if we get an awful haircut, we would much sooner skip school for a few days than bear the shame of looking a hot mess. That's often why we'll opt to wear a hat or a hood—not out of disrespect or as an attempt to stealthily listen to music but because, chances are, some of us feel utterly embarrassed about our hair in the moment. Or it's simply a comfort thing. Upper elementary has some weird moments. Middle school is hard enough! High school can be hell. Imagine having to go through the trauma of a bad hair week on top of that.

I remember being thirteen years old and a freshman at my new high school. I was small with a big and uniquely shaped head—and that's putting it nicely. Thus, I was self-conscious and insecure. Every day, I wore a different hoodie and attempted to keep my hood up for as long as possible to hide my head from others. My business teacher was cool about it. I could tell that he saw me and that he saw my issue. Furthermore, he felt the need to care for me, so he let the hood slide. I felt safe in his classroom, and I will never forget that.

Unfortunately, that environment does not exist everywhere. In most schools, the head-gear police are on patrol, ready to uphold the rules and regulations instead of protecting the social, emotional, and mental well-being of their students. And it's not just with rules about wearing hats—you can substitute that policy with dozens of others that are intentionally set against your students of color (dress codes, uniform policies, discipline policies, etc.).

Be *that* teacher who sees their kids as human and goes out of their way to look past certain rules that might harm them. Is that hat preventing my students from engaging in the lesson? No! My question is this: Are they here and ready to learn? Yes! Of course, I'm for safety, but I'm also for each kid feeling as safe as possible. Even if your school doesn't allow hats or hoods, your classroom can. You can be a haven for those students who need them. You can help end the cycle of policing Black and brown bodies in this small way.

Here is another question I'd like you to reflect on: As you consider the rules and policies at your school, are there any you can identify that specifically target students of color or continually impact them? Are there ways you and others can disrupt these rules and get them changed or dropped?

How Do You See the System?

Systems make up our society. From healthcare to banking to education and, unfortunately, even the prison-industrial complex, American life functions structurally. What's worth noting is how a majority of people (i.e., white people) operate comfortably within these systems with very little strain or stress, while others (i.e., people of color) do not. I recognize that as a Black man, the system, whatever it might be, has not been set up to help me but rather to hurt me. Teachers, this reality leads me to question if the systems, rules, and the culture of our schools have been set up to help or hurt children of color. Unfortunately, I know the answer. I think you do, too.

As a result of my natural aversion to systems, I often request that others "people" me. I'm asking to be seen as a person, not as a representative of a group. When you "people" someone, you are choosing to see past the system in which they fall, past similar circumstances with others, and into their specific scenario. Your vantage point of them is individualized, giving you the opportunity to care for them in a more personal way. Educators, don't we do this with individualized education programs and 504 plans? Doesn't this happen when we make modifications or accommodations for individual students? This personalization, or "peopling," should also happen when we consider how we see our students, particularly those who are Black and brown, and choose to serve them.

When you "people" your scholars, you are treating them ethically and with dignity today, and not based on precedents set by someone else's yesterday. And definitely not on someone's yesteryears. You're making a judgment about what is, not what could have been. That's equity.

So I ask, Do you "people" the students in your classroom? Or are you engaging with them according to the system? According to the rules? According to how others have done it, or how things have always been done? Abandon that! Be *that* teacher who rejects what the system tells them to see and instead sees their kids as what they most authentically are—human.

Here are a few more questions I'd like for you to consider: Would you say that you "people" the students in your classroom or run them through the system? If you intentionally "people" your kids, what does that look like? Can you explain the difference between a system and "the system?" Are all systems bad or harmful?

Do You See the Misinformation?

It's a big job we have to dismantle, piece by piece, a racist system that has privileged some and disadvantaged many others. But as you will continually hear me say, information is a pathway to empathy—the more accurate the information we have to work with, the better informed we'll be to serve others. That said, I see racism as a mix of ignorance, hatred, and misinformation. Racism, in part, is a misunderstanding of the truth about who people are. Let me be clear, information is often purposely distorted to be weaponized against others. That is disinformation, which is intentionally used to confuse, control, and compel those who hear it to act in adherence to fear and hate. But the humanity piece is missing regarding misinformation, pushing folks to move without empathy and respect for others. That's why schools, like most institutions in our society, punish Black and brown kids for simply existing.

But it doesn't stop there. Misinformed kids grow up to become misinformed adults. They grow up to become racist teachers. They grow up to deny Black and brown people loans or housing, or they cross the street when they see a Black or brown man coming their way. *Misinformed* may even be too soft a word because these same misinformed individuals who perpetuate these systems are the ones who kill Black and brown people because *they choose not to see their humanity* at a traffic stop or when they see a Black boy on a walk with a hoodie on or when a Black man is on a jog. This misinformation is a matter of life and death.

That is why these issues matter *now*, in the classroom, because they always matter outside of the classroom. Folks do a lot of passing off in education. "They'll get to that next year," people say. But on issues of race, there might not be a next year. There's right now, this moment. Be *that* teacher who takes care of this issue today.

> On issues of race, there might not be a next year. There's right now, this moment.

In what ways can you take care of race issues in your classroom today? What topics or uncomfortable conversations can you broach with your students and your staff mates? How can you better inform yourself so that you can have these much-needed talks?

We Must See the Struggle

When students of color come into a space, they must work hard to survive in that space, even in ways that they may not be consciously aware of. I am keenly aware of all the work I need to do in certain spaces. As a sheer means of survival, I am conscious of making sure to look friendly and unthreatening, never angry. In an encounter with a police officer, I make sure that my hands are always clearly visible because I know just how high the stakes are if that officer gets jittery around me.

What actions do you think your students of color are considering while they engage with you? Are they afraid to make one wrong move or say something that you might perceive as disrespectful? Are they forced to ask themselves how biased and misinformed *you* are? "Is this teacher one of *them*?" They might think. "Does my teacher see me as *me* or as a caricature?" May their hearts quickly be quieted by realizing that they know their teacher sees them as them. That they're human in your classroom. That they belong there.

How Do You See Yourself?

So how does this all play out in your classroom? As you contemplate the views you hold, look into the mirror. Is the reflection something that pains you or makes you proud of the mindset shifts and personal heart work you've done? To me, that depends on how you choose to see your students and the system everyone is in. Are you taking steps to ensure that outcomes are equitable for all scholars, regardless of how you feel about them? If it's the same offense, what is your response to Emilio and what is your response to Emily? How does your bias play into that? These issues can be tender and sensitive things to look at, but we must examine ourselves first! It all starts with how we honestly see ourselves. Then, and only then, can we work to change how we see our students. This reflection will inevitably improve our classrooms and schools.

And let me be clear, there is much more to the conversation about race in the classroom than can be covered in any one chapter of a book. But, beginning with the belief that everyone is of equal worth and investigating the ways in which we may be communicating otherwise (even inadvertently) in our classrooms is a good first step. There are plenty of excellent books on antiracism that you can read, which should be required reading for educators. Be *that* teacher who builds a pathway toward antiracism starting from inside their classroom.

Reflections

What biases might students *think* you hold about them and why? (e.g., boys vs. girls, quiet learner vs. more expressive, well-behaved vs. more in need of support, Black vs. white, etc.). How can you upend these biases and confirm to your students that they're being treated equitably?

_____

_____

_____

_____

As you consider the rules and policies at your school, are there any you can identify that specifically target students of color or continually impact them? Are there ways you and others can disrupt these rules and get them changed or dropped?

_____

_____

_____

_____

Would you say that you "people" the students in your classroom or run them through the system? If you intentionally "people" your kids, what does that look like? Can you explain the difference between a system and "the system?" Are all systems bad or harmful?

In what ways can you take care of race issues in your classroom today? What topics or uncomfortable conversations can you broach with your students and your staff mates? How can you better inform yourself so that you can have these much-needed talks?

All children develop
at their own pace

They learn from experience,
with time and with grace

So let them be little,
until they get big

Cause grown-ups should be grown,
and kids should be kids

CHAPTER 6

Let Kids Be Kids

Many of our schools don't consider the needs of childhood because many adults can't see things the way kids see them. Naturally, children are filled with faith, innocence, and joy. They view the world through a lens of wonder and possibility, not one marred by life's worst experiences. Most adults don't think this way, and understandably so. But imagine if we did choose to see things how kids do? What if the grown-ups were beaming with expectations for what good the world could bring? If we chose to hope like children, more schools would be filled with the hope of children.

This is where intentional folks like us come in. We can be hopeful for our students. We can decide to be the mentor, the educator, the safe adult, the grown-up, to be *that* teacher who understands what it means to let kids be kids.

Don't get me wrong, as leaders, we are not above children, or better than them in any way, because we're older than them. Though we might know more than them, or different things than them, the mature response to a kid's childhood is to be present with them, to guide them, and to respect their dignity along the way. That's what it means to humanize them and see them as equals in our shared humanity.

But don't get it twisted: I'm not calling for any of us to be a kid, per se. Those days are over. I'm simply encouraging us all to slow down and see the world as would a child. Even Jesus urged his followers to "take the lowly position of [a] child," and they would be considered, "the greatest in the kingdom of heaven."[1] I don't know about y'all, but I'm trynna follow the Good Lord and be great!

Why Won't We Let Kids Be Kids?

Exceptional educators make sure kids can be kids. But with this in mind, it makes me wonder why our educational systems work so hard to make children grow up.

Think about the standard rules in many school settings: sit down, sit still, be quiet, don't call out, line up straight. Now think about how hard that can be for a lot of young people. Why would we set up a system that stamps out the very enthusiasm and exuberance that is one of the best things about childhood? The answer is probably capitalism, ageism, and a few more -isms I can't think of right now. But maybe it's for adult comfort. Noise and movement can be a lot to handle all day long. Maybe it's for compliance. Teaching kids to listen just for the sake of it means some adults can manage (i.e., control) them a lot easier. Whatever the reason, the policing of bodies and restriction of movement do not help children learn and are not best practice.

At the end of the day, too many school rules look to snuff out childhood, exploration, and, to be honest, innocence. Not to be dramatic, but I often think about the overlap between some of these rules and those of prisons. In both, you have to do exactly as you're told or face severe punishment. In both, your movements are restricted and led by those in charge. In both, consequences for mistakes can be steep. *We're talking about kids, y'all.*

Let me be clear: I'm all for safety and support, but totalitarian control over anyone, especially a child, is not a game I'm willing to play. If there is one group in our society who need the freedom, grace, and room to make and learn from mistakes, it's our young people.

---

1   Matt.18:4

Unfortunately, school as we know it does not usually provide that for them. Everything in my soul despises this! Kids should have all the opportunity in the world to simply be kids. Full stop. I especially feel this way about Black and brown children.

The educational system and society at large are particularly tough on Black and brown kids. Too many among us don't want to let children of color have a joyful childhood. The idea of them experiencing joy disgusts them. An experience I've had of this reality occurred when I took my class on a field trip to The Griffin Museum of Science and Industry in Chicago.

On the day of the trip, my scholars were busy exploring and rushing from exhibit to exhibit. At that time, I taught on the West Side of Chicago, and almost all of my students were Black. I imagine the usual ethos on class trips for children of color is stay close to the teacher, don't touch anything, and don't make any noise. But that kind of thinking doesn't fly with me. With the proper safety precautions in place, I never want to restrict my scholars' enjoyment of the world around them. So, yes, they were buzzing from spot to spot. Yes, they were making plenty of noise. Fam, they're kids.

When we got into the mirrored maze, they were lively, laughing, pointing, and passing from mirror to mirror to see themselves displayed big and small. It made my heart happy to see them so engaged, so joyful, so lit up with the experience. It was then that I caught sight of a white couple looking on disapprovingly and muttering under their breath. What I heard was, "Why are *they* so loud?" Fortunately, my kids didn't catch it and went on having a good time. But it made me reflect on the expectation many have that kids should be seen and not heard, especially Black and brown kids. It made me think of the weight of those expectations over time, in which children learn to dial down their natural kid-ness based on the disapproval and judgment of adults. Field trips should be about exploration! Classrooms and school halls should be about exploration! Who are we to dictate how kids explore and how loud and vibrant they should be while exploring?

Instead of feeling shame or telling my students to quiet down, my impulse was to let them have even more fun. To resist in joy! To rebel! I was tempted to tell them to turn it up all the more! But I kept it cool, I let them continue joyfully as they were, and we kept it pushin'.

Student Choice and Student Voice

On another occasion, I was taking first graders to the zoo. I've been on my own class trips as a student where we moved in a regimented way from exhibit to exhibit, from point A to point B, as the adults deemed fit. But this time, I wanted things to be different. I wanted my kids to make plans for themselves, simply because they should have the right to do so. A week before the trip, I shared a map of the zoo with my firsties and explained which exhibits were available to see. As a group, they decided where they wanted to visit.

On the day of the trip, we arrived at the zoo at about 10:30 a.m. Immediately, the Rainbows (the name they chose for themselves) started asking to eat their lunch. Problem was, lunch wasn't scheduled until noon. But they were persistent and vocal enough that it made me stop and think. Who was I to decide when they should be hungry? I explained that if they ate at this hour, they may get hungry later, and Mr. Reed wasn't stoppin' to use his money to buy a bunch of junk food, but they insisted. So, we paused at a few benches and had lunch first thing. Cheetos and turkey sandwiches for second breakfast. Yum! In that scenario, the kids needed to be in control, and I needed to surrender the idea that everything was either my way or the highway.

Although this comes from my own personal outlook on who should control situations in educational settings, the scholarly research in this arena is also moving in this direction.[2] I want to be *that* teacher who encourages his kids to speak up, to think for themselves, and to make informed decisions that benefit them and their community.

---

2 Yong Zhao, *World Class Learners: Educating Creative and Entrepreneurial Students* (Thousand Oaks, CA: Corwin Press, a Joint Publication with the National Association of Elementary School Principals, 2012).

This can only happen when student choice and student voice, no matter how young the kids, are met with teacher encouragement and teacher support.

This can be a tough shift to make in systems that are built on rules, policies, and test scores, though. As an educator, you may not have complete freedom to let your kids be kids as much as you'd like. We can't all just do what we want. Let me be crystal clear, I'm not advocating for permissiveness or lawlessness. But when you allow this shift to happen within you—this inner belief that kids are exploring and growing at exactly the pace that's right for them—then you can find ways to work even within the most restrictive of systems to support and encourage those scholars to be free. That's where the magic is! Everyone has the opportunity to get in on this. It is both free and freeing to let kids be kids.

"But What About the Rules?"

I've heard enough opinions on letting kids be kids that I know many of the arguments against it. What if there's chaos? Does this mean we get rid of all rules? What if kids make the wrong choices? Isn't our whole job to guide them? Here's my take on those questions and valid concerns:

When people ask me, "But won't there be chaos?" my honest response is, "There may be. But we'll make it through." Often, adults are too concerned about chaos and disorder, but I bet this stems from a belief that everything will fall apart without a fixed hand. This thinking demonstrates a lack of trust in ourselves, our students, and in everything we've already put into place. It's like a civil engineer building a bridge then refusing to walk across it. They don't trust their own work. That makes no sense. May this never be the case for you!

We educators must believe in what we do, and expect that work to succeed. Our classrooms don't need to be fixed and immovable. They should be firm, fair, and flexible. When expectations have been set and procedures have been practiced persistently, trust in those measures.

Believe in what you've done. And as routine kicks in, or you deliver reminders and redirections, know that things won't go too far off the rails. You've planned and prepared for this, friend. A little chaos won't cause everything to crumble. The bridge we build might wobble when the winds of a typical school day start to blow, but it *will* remain secure. Walk it! And to truly show your belief, don't be afraid to run across it *with* your kids!

Another objection I often hear is that allowing kids more choice means getting rid of all rules. Of course, we can't have a classroom without rules, as they're commonly thought of. I'm not suggesting that. Many rules can serve their purpose depending on the setting. What I am suggesting, however, is that we be mindful of the reason for every rule. Is the rule in place because it's how things have always been done? Is it there because some of our tremendously expressive kids can be a lot to handle? Is it because the adults just want peace and quiet, or better yet, demand compliance? These are not good reasons. Rules should only be in place if they can be justified and they serve and protect everyone.

When reminding a kid about a rule (i.e., a norm or expectation), I will always give my reasoning or an answer to why, even if they don't ask it. Even though they are children, they deserve to know. Information is an equity issue. I consider it fair for them to be fully informed about the rules they're being asked to follow. Sharing the rationale behind rules is not only an equitable move but also a proactive strategy that begins long before there are any issues to address. Let me explain.

> Information is an equity issue.

When I meet new students, one of the first things we do together is co-construct a set of class-wide expectations. Notice I said expectations, not rules. Rules come from the top down and are stipulations adults create that kids must abide by. However, expectations are a set of guidelines everyone considers together and works toward committing themselves to. This is a more equitable approach to classroom management (i.e., support). I don't say, "Children, welcome to the new school year, these are our rules." I say something more like, "Let's talk about what everyone is looking to get out of our time here in this space." Then we go from there. Comments, questions, discussions, then expectations.

Some of those questions include, What does safety look and feel like to you? How can we keep everyone safe? What might be some possible harmful actions we need to acknowledge, address, and correct in this space? Who might be harmed by these actions and in what ways? How would you define respect? What are some ways everyone can feel heard and respected? What is a boundary? Why is it important to respect other people's boundaries?

These are just a few of the many questions that we'll go through at the beginning of a school year, but the outpouring of our collective responses begins to inform the class-wide expectations we eventually adopt. With this approach, power shifts away from top down, and the kids realize their status as equal stakeholders in their classroom experience. Then, since most of us have collaborated to create these expectations, most agree to them and commit to following them in the interest of everyone's safety, fun, and success.

Now *that* rules! (See what I did there?)

So, when it comes time to discuss behavior, I rarely say, for example, "Don't run in the hallway." Instead, I say, "The expectation we agreed upon is to walk in the hallway." The latter takes literally one extra second to communicate yet provides much more room for understanding. And in the long run, changed dispositions actually save time. In some cases, I'll follow up with, "Because if we're running, we might not see someone coming around the corner in time, and we might bump into them and hurt them." I process the why of the expectation with them so that they can understand the reason for it being in place. Children deserve an explanation for everything. I don't give a lecture, just a quick reminder. Sometimes, it's met with an eye roll on their part, but I'm fine with that. Just because many expectations are good, doesn't mean kids will always immediately see them as good. And it's not that I hate fun! Part of my job is making sure everyone understands what fun looks like in a safe way. Simply put: if we are unwilling or unable to answer the why of a rule, that is a rule we should consider revising or removing.

Choices to Be Made

When people ask me what happens if kids make the wrong choices, again, I think this concern comes from not giving kids enough credit to do what's best for themselves. Sure, as adults, we've got more experience. Sure, we know that if we have our lunch at 10:30 a.m. instead of noon, we may get hungry toward the end of the trip. But the chances are high that we learned this through experience and reflection, not just by being told. The natural consequences (in this case, hunger) taught us, not being scolded by the adults in the room (or at the zoo). We were happy to eat our food earlier than planned, then we dealt with being hungry. And guess what? We learned. It is perfectly fine to let kids learn this way, within reasonable limits.

Children develop self-regulation when they are given the chance to make choices for themselves. Over time, they'll learn to make choices that are good for them for reasons that are important to *them*, not just because they've been told what to do. It may take a while, and it may look messy while it's happening; but it's important to trust and respect kids, along with their why, as they move through their lives. Every choice you think children should make is not always the best choice for them to make. Educators must be humble enough to admit this and operate based on this mindset.

I get really passionate on our role as guides for our students. As I said before, much of education as it exists today is based on a top-down approach where kids are seen as something to mold and perfect. Yes, we have a good and righteous desire to see positive change reflected in our students, but we must not mistake, miscalculate, or centralize our role in their evolution. We don't control that change. We are not in charge of it. Educators are blessed to come along and be a part of the process, but we are not the focus of it. That sounds like God's work. But we are not gods, we're guides.

Just like a highly qualified docent at the city museum, we lead the way, but we should never get in the way. We don't get to control who learns what or the pace at which they learn. We usher them into different spaces, give them our insights and feedback, and watch them grow on their own terms. Oh, and sometimes we get to share a super interesting story about this exhibit or that artifact. That is the work of a good, intentional guide. May we be the same for our students!

To leave you with one final anecdote, I'll tell you the story of Dahlia, a scholar I had in my first year of teaching. She's a great kid with a passion for learning and a lot of enthusiasm. One day, she asked for a hall pass. "Can I take five, Mr. Reed?" I told her, "You got it!" I let her go without giving it a second thought. Thing is, she was out for longer than I expected, so eventually, I poked my head out the door to see if she was around. As part of a display on our hallway wall, there was a huge mirror. Guess who was in front of it, dancing and watching herself move? The dazzling Dahlia!

Here I ask you: Who among us hasn't had a moment when they just needed to dance?

In that instance, I had a choice. I could allow that joy to be, or I could say something to snuff it out. I could be a jerk and shame her for wasting time and not getting back to class promptly, or I could smile to myself and walk back into the room knowing she'd soon follow. Who knew what was happening in Dahlia's life or mind that she wanted, or needed, to experience the joy of movement? Regardless of how anyone else might have felt about it, she needed that moment, and I got out of the way to let her have it. Great educators are always looking for ways to multiply the joy we see in the life of our students. We simply must let kids be kids.

Grow Them, but Don't Make Them Grown-Ups!

> Great educators are always looking for ways to multiply the joy we see.

Teachers have the responsibility to protect children throughout their childhood and to provide them with the space to experience the joy and delight of being a kid. There is absolutely no need for them to grow up. There will be plenty of time for them to act, think, and behave like adults later, when they're adults. We should get away from the adultification of our kids because it harms them, hurts them, and holds them back from genuine growth.

For now, we should focus on helping kids get the most out of childhood, explore, learn from mistakes, and appreciate their innocence. Be *that* teacher, the one who helps cultivate amazing attributes in kids because you see them as kids and support their efforts as kids. Our scholars deserve to be free. Let's let kids be kids!

Reflections

Why is it valuable to educators to think from the perspective of the children they are serving? Do you find it difficult to think about situations from the vantage point of the kids you teach? If so, how might that be a barrier to your relationship-building potential with your students?

What's the difference between raising and guiding kids, and trying to grow them up? Have there been ways in which you've tried to grow kids up or make them conform to adult expectations or standards? How can you change this?

What do you think about your relationship as an adult with the children you serve? Deep down, do you feel like you're better than them or above them? Educators must exhibit a certain humility in our teaching and service of children.

How would you describe the rules in your classroom or school space? Is your approach to rules collaborative and community-based or is your philosophy top down in nature? What kind of changes need to be made?

In what ways do you encourage student voice and student choice in your classroom? Where might there be room for growth?

Who controls your classroom? Elaborate. Who should be in control of your classroom? What benefits are there to the idea of control? What drawbacks are there? When you consider the power dynamics in your classroom, what comes to mind?

Why do children deserve an explanation for every rule, policy, expectation, or consequence? What happens when kids don't receive information or explanations about decisions that involve them?

In what ways are you seeing to it that your students' experience their highest joy and satisfaction with life and their educational experience? Can you think of any ways to ramp up these efforts?

_____

_____

_____

Yes, teachers teach, but
we also need to learn,

Learn to listen well, and
show grace in return

Model being humble,
so our kids can walk the same

If it's about learning,
then teachers lead the game!

CHAPTER 7

The Teacher as the Lead Learner

While I'm certain we give our all to teaching, I often wonder if we're all in when it comes to learning. At least for myself, I ask if I'm leading the pack in seeking knowledge. Are my students confident about *my* thirst for learning? I use the term *learning* broadly here. I'm not talking about getting degrees. That's dope and might get you a little mo' money in ya paycheck, but that's not what I mean. Learning isn't even just poring over academic articles or scholarly journals every morning while you have your coffee. Nah.

I see learning as more of an attitude than an action, or a set of actions. It's a disposition of discovery. Learning is the perpetual search for and acceptance of new and true information, context, or nuances that may be helpful to you in the present or the future. It can be names, numbers, and dates, or it can be an openness to hearing differing viewpoints about those names, numbers, and dates. That's learning, and we can all stand to learn.

Do You Love Learning?

With that said, I ask you to consider the following questions: Do you love to learn? Are you open to gaining new insights and perspectives from other people or educators? Here's a big one: do you actually listen at the district-wide professional development sessions, or are you rolling your eyes every few seconds and working on something else while the presenter speaks? As a teacher, it's not just enough to be phenomenal at teaching. In order to be *that* teacher, we must be willing to take the lead on being taught.

Learning is the willingness to be educated by anyone, anywhere, under any circumstance, and especially by our students. Is this how you see it? Could you be characterized by your love for learning in this way? Do your colleagues and scholars know you as the educator with an attitude bent toward openness, discovery, and change? Or might you be the school's know-it-all, stuck in your ways, and closed off to anything different? Let's find out.

Do you feel like you're often the smartest person in the classroom or the meeting?

Does it bother you when your coworkers ask so-called basic questions that, according to you, they should already know the answer to?

Do your degrees, certifications, and awards make you feel better than others or more deserving of others' respect?

Do you readily accept advice or criticism from others around you? What about from those who are younger or less experienced than you?

Does your five, ten, or twenty years as an educator make you think, "Oh, I already know all of this? They had something like this years ago. Same thing, new serial number."

Do you often say or think to yourself, "I'll just keep doing things my way," instead of considering a new way to do things?

When a student asks you a question you don't know the answer to, do you admit you don't know it or do you try to cover up for your lack of knowledge?

Is it difficult for you to take accountability for your actions or words that negatively impact others?

Do people approach you with new ideas, or do they typically bring them to someone else because they know you won't accept them?

If the answer to any of these questions is yes, my friend, it might be time for a heart check. You might be an educational know-it-all, and quite frankly, can't nobody tell you nothin'! This is not a good place to be—but you *can* change if you want to.

The most effective teachers commit themselves to being teachable. Coachable. Ready to shift and grow whenever they become aware of new, useful information. If this is not your mindset, many around you will miss out on their own development because of you. It is not fair to kids when the adults educating them think they know everything. We have to be willing to learn.

Characteristics of a Lifelong Learner

So, we've become familiar with some of the characteristics of a know-it-all, but what about the characteristics of a learner? I've detailed four main ways that showcase a teacher who is dedicated to learning: learners listen, they give grace, they humble themselves, and they choose to learn from everyone.

Learners Listen

The most important quality needed for a learner is the willingness to listen. It's been said that we have two ears and one mouth for a reason, and I wonder how much more we'd grow as teachers if we listened twice as much as we spoke.

But it can be hard accepting what someone else has to say, especially when it doesn't perfectly align with our own beliefs. Just look at the comment section for pretty much any social media post. It's almost like we're built to close our ears, open our mouths, and disagree. We spend a ton of time cultivating our point of view, then entrenching ourselves in it. So hearing things that go against our polished and practiced perspectives can be difficult or downright impossible.

Let me ask—what happens in your mind when someone comes along and disagrees with your beliefs? When a coworker hits you with, "Well, actually . . ." or "Yeah, but . . ." At that point, are you still eager to learn? To learn from *them*? Do you sit there nodding and wearing an accepting smile, or do you start to get hot? Does imaginary steam start to shoot from your ears, or is your immediate thought to thank them for adding their input? Be honest.

Or what if a parent suggests a way of doing something you hadn't considered yet, or that you're convinced won't work? Do you sit and ponder what they've presented, contemplating whether there's any truthfulness or validity to their statements, or do you become hardened and closed off to what they've said? "Ah, they don't know what they're talking about. Let *me* be the teacher," you think to yourself.

The crux of this chapter lies here: don't see someone's difference in opinion or point of view as a challenge to you. Instead, see it as an opportunity to refine or reform your beliefs. Their differences can be crucial for your growth and development. When we listen, we stand to learn tremendously from outlooks different than our own. While we certainly don't have to agree with everything said or accept everything presented, we would do well to simply hear things out. Being a lifelong learner means being a lifelong listener. There's no way around that.

> Being a lifelong learner means being a lifelong listener.

Learners Give Grace

Another key characteristic of a lifelong learner is giving grace. Too often, kids are greeted with shame from their teachers for negative actions or behaviors that happened in the past—the hour, the class, or the day before. Instead of forgiving that student and forging a path together based on accountability and high expectations, some teachers will hold the poor decision over that kid's head until they feel a lesson has been learned. Or worse, that teacher will decide that the mistake is who the child is and will continue to respond to them based on past actions.

They are still trying to teach at that moment, instead of trying to learn. Grace is missing.

What if we did things differently, though? What if each day we crossed paths with our students, we chose to acknowledge their growth since we last interacted with them? The hope is that they've been reformed by the natural consequences of their actions or refined by the wise perspectives given to them by you and others. The assumption is that they've learned something, so why can't we learn along with them? Can't teachers trust that their students have grown—no matter how much—and treat them accordingly? That's grace!

Instead of seeing them *as* the mistake, we can all learn from their mistake. They can learn how to redo things the next time, and we can learn how to appreciate their new selves. This grace-filled approach would make a world of difference in any classroom.

What if each day, each moment, and with each new breath, we meet our students with grace? What if we choose to have a short memory of the bad and hold onto the vision of their future good? This would completely revolutionize our schools and rehumanize the relationships our scholars have with their educators. Showing grace is what true learning looks like!

C'mon, somebody! I know I'm preachin'!

Don't you like the feeling of forgiveness? Don't you wish you had a clean slate whenever you messed up? Aren't second chances your favorite ones? Doesn't a fresh start sound fantastic anytime it's offered? Teachers, our students feel the exact same way. The children in your life want to experience grace. They need to. Learn to give them some.

When we learn that our students are different each time they return to us, we should treat them differently. Our kids benefit whenever we see them as better than they were before, and so do we! They rise to the occasion whenever we hold out hope for their evolution. Instead of holding yesterday over their head, show them grace and help them look ahead to their tomorrow. That's true teaching, and more importantly, learning!

Here are a few ways to show grace to our students:

- Only bring up past failures when talking about their growth from them, then celebrate the growth!
- Be slow to speak, quick to listen, and quick to forgive.
- If they show up late, say something like, "I'm happy you made it," or "Class is better when you're here!"
- Give instructions again. Yes, again.
- Quickly give them the opportunity to rewind and make things right.
- Swap out taking things away from them for asking them to add something (to the class, the conversation, or the community).
- Tell them stories about famous, successful people who tried and failed before succeeding and ask them to reflect on those stories.
- Share stories of your own failures, what you learned, and how that led to subsequent successes.

> Instead of holding yesterday over their head, show them grace and help them look ahead to their tomorrow.

Learners Humble Themselves

Another key quality of lifelong learners is humility. Pride is no good in the classroom. Be proud of yourself, yes, but never be full of yourself. You must maintain a belief that there's always something more to learn and often more than one way of looking at things. Even when discussing a topic you're well versed in, approaching the topic with a sense of wonder and a willingness to learn keeps the lesson fresh and fulfilling for everyone. This comes in handy especially on the fiftieth time you have to teach drawing inferences or improper fractions, or when you have to make the American Revolution interesting to a new batch of students. There's always new information to share or new ways to share it.

Humility also makes us approachable. We should want folks to feel like they can come to us at any time with anything because they're confident they won't be shamed, shunned, or shooed away, especially our kids. They should know they belong among us and deserve to share our space. It's their space, too. This environment of belonging is built through humility.

I was tutoring a fifth grader named Brandy during my prep one day (cause you know, do we ever truly get a prep?). Brandy was one of those kids the system had let down in so many ways. She'd been forced to be grown and care for her little brother. I found out that she'd experienced multiple traumatic events by the age of ten and, as a result, was constantly moving from house to house. In her previous school years, she regularly found herself being put out of the classroom and in the principal's office due to her behavior. There was little to no stability in her life. According to the world, Brandy just didn't really fit anywhere.

As we came across a vocabulary word—aspire—she asked me what it meant. I defined the word, then gave an example of someone I aspired to be like, Dr. Martin Luther King Jr. Then I asked, "Is there anyone you aspire to be like, Brandy?" Without hesitation, she blurted out, "*You*, Mr. Reed!" After dropping a quick tear (in my heart), I replied, "And why is that?" Her response floored me. She said, "Because you make me feel like I'm supposed to be here." Brandy, like all of us, had been searching for acceptance and had found her place of belonging in the classroom that I was blessed to humbly serve in. Let it be made clear: humility begets belonging.

Learners Learn from Everyone

One of the last characteristics of a lifelong learner is choosing to learn from everyone. Every person in this world has something they can teach us. This goes for our colleagues, the administrator we don't particularly care for, the annoying folks on social media, the caregivers of our scholars, and yes, even our kids. Listening to our students is some of the best professional development there is. The children in our classrooms have a wealth of knowledge and lived experiences different from our own which we can learn from if we choose to. And since we spend the most time with them, it would make the most sense to soak up everything we can from them.

Traditional models of education come from the mindset that the teacher has the power, the control, and all the information, and that the responsibility falls solely on us to lead the children. While we can certainly provide rich experiences that give scholars the opportunity to explore new ways of thinking, we can't do it all. No one needs that. What we need is to have the humility to let others teach us things we wouldn't ever expect to be taught.

Like how to dance! My kids are always dancing—in their seats, as they grab supplies, while standing in line for lunch, while waiting for instructions, in the hallway, on the bus during a field trip. They're literally always dancing. Dance is a form of communication and joyful expression! When my students show me their dance moves, they're inviting me to two-step right into their world.

Sure, I know I don't look my best when I'm trying to replicate the latest social media moves. Nine times out of ten, I probably look goofy as heck, but I don't care. I know I won't be going on any Soul Train lines any time soon. But whenever I humble myself and try something I'm not great at, I exemplify for the kids a person who is willing to learn and do something new, even if they look foolish at first. They get the chance to be the teacher, offering me their knowledge and expertise; but my example of humble learning teaches them, as well. When we take on this way of looking at our role, kids feel trusted, empowered, and safe to learn, too.

We've probably all heard young people lament, "Nobody listens to kids." But we get to be *that* teacher who shows them there is someone who listens—us! There's a reciprocity there. Kids listen to adults who listen to kids. They feel a sense of accomplishment when they've been heard and can teach the adults something.

> **Kids listen to adults who listen to kids.**

And do you remember that time when you finally learned that dance your students taught you and their excitement was through the roof when you nailed it? You loved that feeling, didn't you? So did your kids! That's what choosing to learn from everyone can produce!

How to Cultivate Lifelong Learning

As with anything else, a heart for lifelong learning can be developed. You don't have to remain stuck with just what you know now. You can grow! Humans are meant to be mobile in our mindsets and should always aim to procure new information that will put us on a path forward. There are three significant ways to build this learning spirit: accept losses humbly, ask for accountability, and apologize regularly.

Accept Losses Humbly

At some point, we are going to lose. It's inevitable. The quicker we come to grips with that reality, the better off we will be. But this realization should inspire us to get ahead of those losses and learn from them. Because I'm imperfect and recognize that failure might be just around the corner, I prepare myself to learn from that failure. I have to, otherwise a loss will have been for nothing. Instead, if I operate with an attitude of discovery, rather than a defensive or disappointed one, I can ultimately win. Instead of thinking I've got it all figured out by myself, I must readily accept that my shortcomings tell me something about myself that I didn't know before.

What positives can I take from this?

What do I need to sit with and learn from?

What growth do I need to experience here?

What can I do differently next time?

Nelson Mandela once said, "I never lose. I either win or learn." We must accept and engage our losses with a heart of humility.

If you are not willing to humble yourself and learn from your loss, you'll lose twice over. First the failure, and then the failure to learn that will lead to more loss. Let me give you an example. If I make the mistake of singling a student out for something in front of the entire class, that child will feel embarrassed and angry with me (and rightfully so!). They'll want to go toe-to-toe with me—it might even evolve into a shouting match. Then I'll lose control of the classroom. That's a clear loss, and I have to take that *L*.

If I'm prideful about failing there, I'll do the same thing the next time, thinking, "It's just that kid. They're just so disrespectful. They just need to learn." The reality is *I* need to learn! Why put myself in the same situation by refusing to admit to my own shortcomings? I'm the one that messed up in that scenario. Why lose twice?

If I'm humble about the situation, I'll realize that addressing a personal matter with a scholar in front of the entire class is harmful and serves neither of us. Instead, after discovering what went wrong, I should pull that kid to the side and address any future concerns privately. This way, they know what I need them to know, they can go handle their business, and no one else needs to be in on it. No shouting, no back and forth, no losses. Be humble whenever you take an *L* and learn from it so that you don't have to take another one.

Ask for Accountability

The next way to cultivate lifelong learning is to ask for accountability. Ask for people to keep you in line with goals that you've shared. While our intentions might be good, there will always be areas we cannot see where we are lacking or come up short. Therefore, help from others is crucial.

Ask your administrators to point out places where you can grow, but be willing to hear them, even when it doesn't feel good. Each year, I ask my principal, "Please tell me what you would consider to be a successful year from me." One year, Principal B. said, "Be coachable, be flexible, be consistent," and I asked her to hold me to that. Was I perfect all year long? No. But knowing there was someone expecting me to execute on what I had committed to helped me stay the course.

Next, ask your colleagues to watch you instruct or listen to an idea you have to give you feedback. Again, both cases might be tough, but the ultimate goal is to make you a better educator. Listen to them as they explain what they saw going on in the back of the room during second period or when they suggest that you *not* turn your back during instruction. Always be willing to learn something others know that you don't know.

And please do not neglect to ask your students to keep you accountable! They are the ones who spend many hours with you every week, so of course, they're going to have one of the most well-rounded classroom views of you. Plus, we all know how kids keep it real, so don't ever worry about them sugarcoating anything.

At the beginning of each school year, I tell my students that I'm a Christian, and for me, that means I keep my language clean in a work setting. I tell them, "If you hear me cuss at any point, call me out, and I'll pay you fifty bucks!" How much do you want to bet that those kids are hanging onto my every word, hoping, wishing, and even praying that I slip up and swear? It's a silly thing we do, but they're keeping me accountable. And there are dozens of other promises I make and expectations I set that my students hold me accountable to. Everyone learns when accountability is the law of the land.

By the way, I have never ended up owing a kid fifty bucks.

Apologize Regularly

One of the final suggestions I'll make to develop an attitude of lifelong learning is to apologize regularly. As humans, we make mistakes often, so it's best to be quick to apologize and to make things right. No one is perfect. None of us has ever spent a single day flawlessly engaged with all our scholars and colleagues. We have been in error in some way or another. We have been curt, said something mean, or insinuated something inconsiderate about someone. We have acted out of anger or embarrassment instead of responding with logic and love. All of us have fallen short and dropped the ball at some point. We have all been in that position before, but one of the most important things is figuring out what to do while we're there.

There are four things we can do to apologize correctly: humbly admit our wrongs, delete our defensiveness, ask for forgiveness, and commit to doing our best the next time.

First, be humble and admit that you are wrong. It costs nothing to be honest, yet everything is in jeopardy whenever we skirt around the truth. The world tells us that those who are prideful are winners, that cheaters get farther, and that liars come out on top. This might often be the case, but as educators, our aim should not be to win at any cost; it should be to become better people and show our students how to do the same. We can do so by humbly accepting due blame.

Next, delete your defensiveness. Don't try to deflect attention away from yourself or minimize the magnitude of your mistake. You did it, so own it. Then overcome it. You're doing no one a favor when you shine the spotlight away from your miscue. Teachers, when you are quick to accept the blame for something you did, your students will learn to do the same!

Third, ask for their forgiveness. Being a learner in the classroom means learning to ask the people you've offended to forgive you. Imagine how humane it makes you look when you ask a child to pardon an adult's offense against them. Doing so levels you out in their mind. It reminds them they have a voice and deserve to be heard. Asking a student to forgive you might compel them to ask the same of the adults or peers in their life.

Lastly, commit to doing better next time. While it's important to do better, it can be equally as important to communicate that commitment audibly. People want to see changed behavior, but they also want to hear the corresponding words, as well. Frame your future with a verbal commitment, then follow through on what you've said.

Let me be the first to admit that I've made a million mistakes as an educator. If there's anyone who should be the spokesperson for messing up in the classroom, it's Dwayne Reed. So please, when you have a misstep, don't believe the lie that you're the only one in the world who has messed up. You're not. There are millions of other human beings who have done the same.

During one class, I noticed that some of the girls were spraying perfume. I explained to them that I didn't want fragrances with potential chemicals to be sprayed in the class because my son, who was a toddler at the time, had severe eczema and allergies. I didn't want to bring home any allergenic substances on my clothes. Later *that* day, I saw two students walking to the back of the room, hiding something. From my peripheral vision, I saw them spray something out—perfume. I called out the name of one of the girls in a louder tone than I normally use. I became frustrated with what I perceived to be blatant disrespect, particularly since I had just explained why this was an issue for me.

It wasn't my best moment as a teacher.

Later in the hallway, I took a moment to speak to her. "I want to apologize to you. I shouldn't have raised my voice at you," I said.

She replied, "I want to apologize to you, too. It was my bad, Mr. Reed. I wasn't even thinking about your son."

I accepted her apology and said, "Thank you for doing the practice of considering others."

If I hadn't found the humility to apologize to her, there wouldn't have been room for her to apologize to me and do the work of becoming more empathetic for others. If I hadn't learned from our classroom interaction that I need to hold myself to a higher standard, there wouldn't have been room for her to do the same outside of the classroom. Normalize apologizing to children.

With all things considered, be *that* teacher who is eager to be taught. To become a lifelong learner, it will take a lifetime of listening, giving grace, and accepting what others have to say. When teachers lead in these efforts, their classrooms are filled with true learning, understanding, and joy.

Reflections

Teachers are some of the smartest people in our society. But with great intelligence comes great responsibility. Do you struggle with being the teacher who thinks they know it all or can do it all?

Which is better: A prideful teacher who knows everything and can do everything themselves, or a humble teacher who has gaps but knows to ask for help? Elaborate.

Why is graciousness a sign of a great teacher? Are you quick to show others, students, or yourself grace? Describe what a school year filled with grace would look like. Describe what a year filled with reminding students of mistakes and holding onto wrongs would look like.

What would it look like in schools if teachers saw students, colleagues, parents, and everyone else as potential teachers? If we saw everyone else as a potential educator?

Define what you think accountability should look, sound, or feel like for a teacher. What should an apology sound like from a teacher to their students? How would more accountability and apologies, especially from the teacher, impact a typical classroom?

Teamwork makes the dream work,
so don't sleep

Many hands make light work,
a clean sweep

Together with your squad,
and you can't be beat!

It's no reach, to declare,
it takes a team to teach!

CHAPTER 8

It Takes a Team to Teach

*I*f you've ever watched one of those inspirational teacher movies, you may have gotten the impression that teaching is about one solo hero making a difference in kids' lives. But if you've been teaching for longer than fifteen minutes, you know that's not the full story, or even half a percent of it. Teaching does take unique, inspiring individuals, that's for sure; but a successful career is unequivocally the result of a team effort. And if you know anything about team sports, you know championship teams are built, not born. It takes vision, hard work, and intentionality to make sure your squad is operating at the top level in pursuit of that chip!

I like to think in terms of a basketball team when I consider how we must all function together to make schools better. I love the sport, both as a player and as a fan. To me, schools are like a b-ball team in a number of ways:

- We have at least one common goal (to win the championship)!
- We work to make sure our individual goals align to achieve our common goal.
- We identify our specific strengths and specialties and embrace them.
- We work together no matter the opposition we face.

We're All in This Together

Do the kids in your class just appear out of thin air when the bell rings? That's the question that comes to mind when I hear some teachers say, "I go in my room, I shut the door, and I teach."

Students come from places, and they're on their way to other places. They don't stay in your classroom forever. They're "yours," but they're not *only* yours. They come from home, Grandma's house, and the K–2 building, and they'll transition to PE, after-school care, and eventually high school or college. Their lives consist of more than just *you*. So, if you don't intentionally work with a team of others to help your students, those children will be deprived of crucial input and insights that you alone cannot provide them. As they say, "There is no *I* in *team*," so closing your door is not the most effective way to educate your students.

Treating your scholars as if they only exist, find their meaning, or derive their joy when they're with you is negligent and self-absorbed. You are not the center of their world, and my friend, you are not the only one on the team. *Pass the ball.*

Two Different Approaches

When I had my first Black teacher in the fifth grade, unfortunately, she wasn't particularly fond of me. So, I can't remember taking much from her. However, that same year, I was introduced to an after-school worker named Ms. Billie. Now Ms. Billie was the best!

Ms. Carter told me to be quiet. Ms. Billie lovingly sang my name.

Ms. Carter couldn't wait for me to be out of her presence. Ms. Billie would light up whenever I came around.

The bottom line is this: teaching as a team acknowledges that our students spend time in spaces beyond our classroom. Thus, we must focus on ways to work together with those who work in spaces beyond our classroom. There are other people who may be better suited to serve our kids in the ways they need. Ms. Billie helped me far more than my fifth-grade teacher did that year; but looking back on it, I wish Ms. Carter would have been open to hearing what Ms. Billie had to say about me. That collaborative effort would have meant everything to me!

Shutting my door and teaching "my kids," won't cut it. The students get cheated that way. As teachers, we need to shift our thinking to where we see "my kids" as collectively "our kids."

I long for the day when every educator opens their classroom door, steps into the hallway, and sees every kid, even the ones not on their class roster, as their own. Whether it's a past student, one you've never had, or a scholar you'll have in the future, we'd do well to consider them part of our collective responsibility to care for. That's teamwork!

Who's on the Team?

Who exactly is on your school's team, and what position do they play? Let's take it to the basketball court for answers.

On a typical basketball team, there are five players in the game at one time, the center, power forward, small forward, shooting guard, and point guard. Just like in education, each person involved is uniquely suited and trained to successfully fulfill their role in hopes of helping their team win. We should strive to build a dream team of educators.

On the real ballcourt, my team would consist of these NBA legends: Shaquille O'Neal (center), Tim Duncan (power forward), LeBron James (small forward), Michael Jordan (shooting guard), and Magic Johnson (point guard). Those five players in the ballgame at the same time would win every single match they played and secure multiple championships. Will this lineup ever happen? Of course not. It's all a dream. But this kind of lineup *is* possible in a school setting. Let me explain.

While we will never see MJ and LeBron on the court at the same time, the folks in our schools can work together to be the GOAT

(Greatest of All Time) and create a dynasty of sensational education experiences. In the school building, this lineup of teammates would consist of these five groups:

- Administrators
- Trusted Adults
- Parents/Caregivers
- Students
- Teachers

The Center: Administrators

The first member of this team is the school administrators. They represent the position of center. Think Shaq. The Big Diesel of the office and the hallways. On paper, administrators are the strongest and most powerful players in the game. They are a force to be reckoned with! As the center, they are the bodyguard of the team and are always willing to fight for and defend the school. Hurrghh!

In a perfect world, superintendents, principals, and other administrators would carry the weight of the school team on their shoulders. They would welcome the responsibility of taking on the thorniest problems that come up and would accept a portion of the accountability if the school and its constituents weren't properly defended. Good administrators with keen awareness, true vision for greatness, and a bent toward excellence can be a tremendous help to the staff who just want to do right by the kids. In fact, great administrators are the reason many teachers stay in the game! And let me be clear—there are lots of great administrators out there! But truthfully, all administrators aren't always great.

Sometimes, just like the center on a basketball team, administrators don't have good court vision, or they can be too big and powerful for their own good. Unfortunately, this can mean they just stand in the way. When this happens, what should the rest of the team do?

Tell the center (your administrators) to *move*!

Of course, this can't be done in a mean or crass way. Even when it happens on the court, the center's teammates aren't aiming to hurt the big guy's feelings or cut him down to size. They're just trying to help the team win! By the same token, telling admin to move isn't about being disrespectful, getting back at our bosses, or being petty; it's about winning.

I'm calling for educators to simply be decent human beings and lovingly point their administrators (*also humans*) toward the goal at hand. Say, "Look, we're all just trying to make plays. We're trying to put the ball in the hoop just like you. Please, scoot over and make way for everyone to do their thing. And who knows, someone might even toss you an alley-oop that you can slam dunk! That's how we'll win this, *together*."

Here's what something like this could sound like in real life:

- "I'm taking my students out for an extra recess right now. I bet they'd love it if you could pop by and play for a few minutes!"
- "No, I can't stay past my contracted hours."
- "Yes, we're watching a movie the day before a major break. Have you seen this one? You're more than welcome to watch with us!"
- "Hey, I'd like for you to push for this again. I really believe our kids need it."
- "No, but I really appreciate that you thought of me."

Move doesn't always mean, "Get out of the way." Sometimes it means, "Hey, get to a better spot so that we can make things happen." With this new understanding, teachers, please do not be afraid to tell your administrators to move. They are not always right; and as a team player, you privately calling them out, publicly (graciously and respectfully) calling them in, and proactively calling them up on certain things serves them, too. Remember, everyone has their biases and blind spots, and good teams address these realities together.

I understand it can be scary, though. Downright terrifying, even! While I've never had a conversation with Shaquille O'Neal, I don't imagine asking him to get out of the way would be one of our easiest discussions. And, keepin' it real, some of us fear our supervisors more than we fear 2002 Shaq in the paint (which is wild if you think about it)!

But, friends, do not be afraid of your boss. Do not fear retribution from them for speaking up for yourselves, your staff mates, or your scholars. Do not fear what might happen if you do the right thing; fear the possibility of regret if you do nothing. I am not sorry for taking my students outside to our school playground that day. I am not sorry about standing up to a bully of an administrator. Yes, it cost me my job, but that was a price I was willing to pay for sticking to my values and principles. I was willing to be *that* teacher. And as those teachers, we must be confident enough to tell our administrators to move.

> Do not fear what might happen if you do the right thing; fear the possibility of regret if you do nothing.

To everyone out there dealing with a bad leader, I empathize with you, having myself dealt with a fair share of them. But I also want to encourage you to fight past any fears you might have and be bold. If you're religious, do it for God. If not, do it for your family or in their honor. Do it for the kids! Above all, do it for yourselves. Be bold enough to believe in you. Take courage and care for yourself. Tell Big Diesel down in the front office to get out of the way! We've got some shots to make!

My final push is this: respect your principal, honor your AP, learn from the superintendent, hold administration accountable, but never fear them. Even if they let you go, there are other schools that would love to have the fiery, focused, and free version of you on their team. And if you're not able to move to another school—which is totally fine—find a compromise or make small moves at the school you're currently in. Speak up! Generate noise so others might join in until you've all made change together! Regardless of your choice, feel empowered to be your authentic, assertive selves, not just in the classroom but also in the main office with the administration. The school team cannot win until educators become courageous enough to tell their admin to move.

A Brief Note to Administrators

Having been both a teacher and an administrator, I can speak from experience when I say admin are such valuable players on the school team. Yes, the bad ones catch a lot of flak (and deservedly so), but the good ones often get lumped in with them, as well. I don't think that's fair. Many administrators are dialed in to their team's needs, open to criticism or feedback, and humble enough to actually move when they hear a teammate say *move*. So those folks are the ones we should be showing love to! The schools that have these kinds of ballers always win big!

So, teachers, if you have a school administrator who is a star, thank them for shining the way they do. If they care for the well-being of every staff member and each child in the school, show them you see that and celebrate it. If they've got a teachers-first mentality and live it out, praise them for administering and leading with empathy and love. If they respect your humanity, make it a point to honor them for being the definition of a team player publicly, and do it frequently.

And to all those administrators out there doing right by their team, thank you.

The Power Forward: Trusted Adults

Our next dream team position is the power forward, represented by the great Tim Duncan. All trusted adults who come into contact with kids fall into this category. That would include, but isn't limited to counselors, secretaries, cafeteria staff, nurses, custodians, after-school tutors, social workers, paraprofessionals, speech language pathologists, classroom aides, and recess coordinators, to name a few.

In basketball, a power forward's job is to get the big things done quickly. With a center, you may hear things like, "This might take a long time since I've gotta run it up the pipeline." Sometimes it takes a while to get things going with the big man. However, with a power forward, problems run into solutions, fast:

"Here's that first aid kit you asked about! Head back into your classroom; I've got this!"

"Those are in high demand, so we keep them tucked over there. Here ya go."

"I'll contact their parents and get back to you about this ASAP."

"I wanted to make sure you knew about this. Do you have any questions for me?"

"Here, allow me to show you how to do this."

"How can I support you?"

The educational power forward is the gasoline of a school's car. Without them, nobody moves. They always ask where they can help or fill in the gaps, then they do it. They address needs immediately and get the job done the right way.

One of Tim Duncan's nicknames was The Big Fundamental, and for good reason. He played the game the right way. He wasn't flashy or boastful. He wasn't fishing for compliments after every shot or aiming for the praise of his peers. He just put his head down and got busy. The trusted adults in our school spaces are like this, too. With them, there's no major theatrics or cutting corners. They've been around the block a few times, so they know what's up ahead; and often, they know the best ways to deal with issues.

It was halfway through my second year of teaching when I felt *done*. (Have you ever been there?) One of our amazing paraprofessionals had apparently been picking up on my frustration and watching me get close to my boiling point. One day after dismissal, as I was walking past a bulletin board he was working on in the hallway, Mr. McGee stopped in me in my tracks:

"Hey, Mr. Reed!"

"Hey, Mr. McGee," I replied quietly.

"I'ma be straight up with you, bro. I can tell you're going through something right now."

I guess my body language said it all.

He then said, "It might not be much, but I want to help you let go of some of that steam. Besides, I need to clear this board anyway. Here, go ahead and rip all the paper off."

Surprised, I exclaimed, "Wait, what? You want me to just make a mess of this thing?"

He said, "Yeah, bro! I can tell you need to let loose a bit. I ain't got no boxing gloves right now, so this is the best I can offer you. Take it. Rip everything down."

When I tell ya'll, I got to rippin' and pullin' and tearin' and just about everything else! I felt like a toddler with a tantrum, and not a single shred of paper stood a chance! It felt so good being able to release my stress in a way that wouldn't harm anyone and that would actually help someone, too.

After this therapeutic moment, I helped Mr. McGee collect the strips of paper that had piled up along the hallway floor. Then, I thanked him for stepping up to help me. For me as a teacher, when these trusted adults come through, it's just as impactful as when the principal comes through. Their presence and their efforts truly make the team tick. I love being able to use the fast, fundamental support of other adults to help children have the best educational experience possible. It takes a team of trusted adults to teach.

I'd be remiss if I didn't share a few ways to show our appreciation for these trusted adults:

- Teachers know how thankless our job is, and it's often just as bad for the other adults around the school. Thank these trusted adults and publicly celebrate their many contributions to the team.
- Refer to every trusted adult as an educator. The moment we identify each person on campus as a facilitator of learning is the moment our kids will realize that each interaction they have is an opportunity to learn.
- Point these educators out—name them. Make the students aware of them, their role, and how greatly they impact the school community.

The Small Forward: Parents/Caregivers

Next up, we have LeBron James holding it down at the small forward position. A small forward's role in the game is to essentially do it all. Whenever they're on the court and the team needs someone to step up, they are eager to do so. Like LeBron, a small forward is versatile and can comfortably play all five positions. The parents and caregivers of our kids fit this description; they are the do-it-alls for their all in all.

Are the parents and caregivers of our students the principal? No. But they can fiercely protect and advocate for their child, one hundred percent! Are the parents and caregivers of our students the secretary or social worker of our school? Not often. But they can be there to support their child at every moment just like those trusted individuals. And that's their strength—their resourcefulness, their flexibility, and their versatility. We, as educators, need to tap into this resource much more often.

When the parents and caregivers of our kids play their role, it can include a little bit of everything. They can take care of business around the school building, be their child's best advocate, and carry on the educational process outside of the classroom. Similar to King James, they're a star both on and off the court. We need these people on our teaching team!

Therefore, I get a jump on recruiting these ballers early on. Before the start of a new school year, I call every parent or guardian for each one of my students. I don't wait for back-to-school night or for challenging behaviors to arise in class later on. Nope, I get their number from the school office and call them right away. My words on that first call usually go something like this:

"Hello, this is Mr. Reed, and I'm excited to be your child's teacher this year."

After a few more introductions and pleasantries, I'll follow up with, "I'd love to visit your family and show you some of what will be going on in class this year. Plus, I want to give you all the opportunity to familiarize yourselves with me. Would you feel comfortable and safe with me visiting before the school year begins?" And that's how it goes. Call it an advanced parent-teacher conference with a super intentional twist.

Now, some parents are delighted with that kind of personalized attention. But let me tell you, not all are. Some ask if we can meet in a place other than their home, which is totally fine, of course. Some say it's not a good time, and, unfortunately, we never get the chance to meet. And more than one parent has cussed me out. "When the [bleep] ya'll start doin' this [bleep]?" one mother said. She and I are pretty good friends, now, so it all worked out in the end. To that point, I don't take any resistance or rejection that I receive personally. Why would I? It's probably got nothing to do with me anyway.

Not My Team, but Ours

A lot of adults have experienced trauma of their own in school (their memories have distorted their ideas about teachers or school in general) or they are parents to a child that hasn't felt good about their educational experience. So, if they're initially hesitant to accept my outreach, I get it. If they're not immediately a fan of me, it's understandable. But as their child's teacher, it's about playing the long game.

A regulation NBA basketball game is forty-eight minutes long. A typical school year is 185 days. That just means, we've got some time, y'all. Even if things are rocky from the start, be patient. There's a lot of basketball left to play. Share your heart with the parents and caregivers of your students and your desire to walk with them over time. The more you inform them, the more opportunities they'll have to relate to you, trust in you, and work with you.

Whichever way a preliminary meeting happens, enrolling parents in their children's experience in your classroom is key to a productive, peaceful year. I have to make caregivers feel like they belong in education, because they do. It's not simply *my* team, it's *our* team. I let them know I'm here to listen to them and work with them. *Not* to do everything they ask me to do, of course, but to do everything I can to best serve their child. That way, if an issue arises, they know that the first and best step to getting it resolved is to get in touch with me. They instinctively know to pass me the ball. And typically, after building this kind of relationship with them, everyone's outlook, attitude, and performance improves. Then we start winning games! Teachers, parents are *not* the enemy; they're your teammates. Pass *them* the ball!

Going back to that initial meeting, for caregivers who are open to it, the agenda is simple. I want to know, What would a successful school year look like for you and your scholar? What are you looking for in a teacher? What are some areas where you or your child weren't served well previously? In what specific ways would you like me to help your student best? Asking solid questions like these always produces a specific set of marching orders to guide my service of an individual child.

I'll give you one example. Early one year, a mother told me, "My son, Damari, doesn't want to speak out loud in the classroom. He has a speech impediment." In that instant, I knew what my personal goal would be for Damari that year. With sensitivity to his feelings, I gave him first private, then classroom-wide opportunities to speak his mind when he felt comfortable. Was he giving TED Talks by the end of the year? No, he wasn't. But did he open up in ways he might not have if his mother hadn't filled me in and allowed me to help him shine? You'd better believe it!

Years after he had been a fifth grader in my classroom, I caught up with Damari at a local park. Ironically, he was one of the loudest dudes on the basketball court, making sure everybody heard what he had to say. Not a keynote speech, mind you, but nobody was gonna stop or slow his words. That's a victory for that student, his mama, and for me.

But hold up, maybe an at-home meet-and-greet is a little bit past your comfort zone. Or perhaps you're a high school teacher or a specials teacher, and there's no possible way you could ever make that many phone calls or visits. Listen, that's totally okay! Work with what you've got and within your style and reach:

- Send a carefully crafted and creative email home introducing yourself.
- Create a short video (or music video) and share it with parents and caregivers.
- Catch Mom, Dad, Grandpa, or Auntie at early morning drop-off or afternoon dismissal and give them your educator elevator pitch.
- Reach out to two or three adults of your students once a week and make it your year-round mission to connect with some of the families of your kids. Over time, it adds up!

Whatever it is, try your best to meet, greet, and speak early on.

Power to the People!

Lastly, I am particularly mindful of empowering parents, especially Black and brown parents. I remind them of the power that they have, not just with their children, but within the school system. Too often, they've been told, "Don't worry, let the professionals handle it." But, to me, there is no greater expert on a child than the people who care for them at home or away from school. They are the experts!

So what does bringing parents into the team look like? They are present in my classroom. They volunteer their time, resources, or expertise to help teach me and the rest of my scholars. Caregivers come on field trips or chaperone school dances or sporting events. I absolutely love hands-on, helicopter, and "Hey, how's everything going" parents! I don't ever get annoyed by the super involved caregiver. That proves to me that they're people who care a whole lot. I'm never going to take that as a threat or see it as a nuisance. The more, the merrier. And for the ones who can't be as visible or involved in the school experience, they're still needed, too! Those adults giving teachers their trust or any insider details about their kids goes a long way.

The quicker we see the parents and caregivers of our students as valuable team members, the quicker we'll succeed as a team in reaching our common goals. One of my favorite sayings is an African proverb, "If you want to go fast, go alone. If you want to go far, go together." All that to say, "Go *team*!"

The Shooting Guard: Kids

The next set of folks who must be viewed and treated as part of our teaching team are young people. An educator who neglects to consider their students as core role players in the classroom commits a crucial mistake. Our scholars are just as significant as every other position on the team, and it could be argued that they hold one of the most important spots on the team. It is *their* education after all.

With that said, kids are the shooting guard of the teaching team, and their legendary representative is none other than Michael Jordan. Why MJ? Cause he's the greatest! And if you're reading this book, you probably believe, like me, that kids are, too.

As the shooting guard, students are always ready to take on anybody standing in their way. They are fierce competitors and hate to lose at anything. Whether it's a kindergartner losing their spot in line, or a senior in high school losing at the math review game, they take it personally, just like a certain number twenty-three.

But while kids are certainly great, they're not perfect. There are areas in their life that need to be called in and coached up. For example, like His Airness, some students can be quick-tempered, boastful, and self-absorbed. Or they can lack empathy for their peers, or act as if they don't care about anything at all, except for winning.

If we're being honest, we all have our shortcomings. And even though our students are the reason we're at school, it's everyone's job to hold the star player—the students—accountable. This means letting them shine but also showing them how to share their light in the most appropriate ways. In addition, accountability means modeling humility for children so that when they face humbling moments themselves, they'll know how to get through them.

Not even Michael Jordan was above humble pie from the start. In his sophomore year of high school, he was five feet, ten inches tall and underdeveloped as a player. And legend has it that he was cut from his school's basketball team. (Turns out this may be part myth, as he was actually just placed on the junior varsity squad to help him develop further as a player.) But we all know what happened years after that: Cut or not, MJ would go on to prove he was cut from a different cloth. That humbling experience placed a chip on his shoulder that he used as motivation to eventually secure six NBA championships.

In addition to humility, it took coaches—and most likely teachers—who believed in him enough to hold him accountable, to help him develop his dynamic skills, and to reach his goals. Teachers, we get to do this!

We've got the next Michael Jordan, Dr. Martin Luther King Jr., or Maya Angelou sitting in our classroom right now! All students are star players in their own way! All students are their very own version of Michael Jordan! No matter what happened before or how they're performing now, they are bona fide superstars. How are you deliberately working to make their stars align? What are you doing to reach their hearts and to help them reach heights they can't even yet imagine? As I've said all along, your heart work here must be intentional.

In many neighborhoods, once the community recognizes that a certain kid can "hoop" and has a shot at going to the NBA, everyone who's invested in that community will come together to protect that child. The hood stands up to make sure their star player is taken care of, and some folks will even pool their limited resources together to provide a way for that kid to "make it." That's intentionality. And that's the kind of service we on the teaching team get to provide for our students. Each of our scholars has the chance to make it, somehow or someway, and we get the opportunity to help make that happen!

When we practice this kind of intentional teaching, we walk beside our kids through adversity. When we choose to be *that* teacher, we encourage our kids to exercise their agency. Being *that* teacher means watching them succeed and prosper abundantly. That's the reward for our role as their educator. Our hard work of coaching the star players somehow always pays off. One day, we'll be somewhere

> **Each of our scholars has the chance to make it, somehow or someway, and we get the opportunity to help make that happen!**

watching our kids shine, proud of them and proud of our own work in their lives.

The Point Guard: Teachers

Lastly, we have the point guard, Magic Johnson, on our team. This role belongs to our teachers. This is us! The point guard is the coach on the court and serves as the floor general—instructing, guiding, correcting, and encouraging. Teachers set the pace and the tempo of the game. We're responsible for setting up the plays and directing the players. In this position, you've got to have great court vision. You have to envision what will happen before it becomes reality. Not like a psychic, but more like a dreamer, a believer. Teachers do the work of casting the vision then doing whatever it takes to help the rest of the team carry that vision out.

Magic Johnson played in the National Basketball Association during the 1980s and early '90s. His team was nicknamed the Showtime Lakers because, led by Johnson, they were flashy, fascinating, and downright fun to watch. Basketball fans simply could not get enough of the men in purple and gold, and Magic was the ringleader of all the titillating action.

Teachers, that's us! Call it magic, madness, or anything in between; but we are the ones at the helm of this thing called education.

Sure, sometimes we can be flashy—dressing up as a character to drive home a lesson or just dressing nicely to show our kids that teachers have swagger, too.

We are unquestionably fascinating! No matter who we are, each of us is different and brings our own, unique personality to the classroom every day. Even though our kids think we're lame at times, they love us for being us!

And lastly, without a doubt, teachers are fun. We gamify our lessons, we speak in goofy voices, we play, and we're not afraid to simply be a big kid at heart.

I have no problem being the magician, waving the wand, and even pretending to be the bunny in the hat if it helps wow my kids with the wonders of education. Have you ever seen the lightbulb go off in a student's head right after you explained the lesson?

Yup, that's magic!

In a game of basketball, on any given possession, a team has twenty-four seconds on the shot clock to put up the ball and try to score. There's an urgency there. In a school year, it's similar. You've got about 185 days to see the goals for your scholars come to fruition. Plus, there are smaller shot clocks along the way, like marking periods or standardized tests or the time until the next holiday or break. Teachers, as the point guard, your job is to create open shots for your players. You do the work of getting everyone else around you in a position to score and to succeed. You run the court. *You* are magic.

The Box Score

As you can see, it truly takes a team to pull off a great education. It takes you, first and foremost, bringing your enthusiasm, your wit, and your creativity. It takes parents and caregivers being fully engaged and communicative. It takes kids being taught to invest in their own learning. It takes the support of your fellow teachers and other trusted adults in the building and the collective wealth of knowledge you've all developed. And it takes an administration to support you and give you the tools necessary to succeed. That's championship teaching. Are you ready to get in the game?

Reflections

We've seen that teaching is truly a team game. What ways can you grow in your collaboration with others as you teach your students?

Not everyone innately has team spirit. Some of us naturally thrive as the lone wolf. Would this be an issue or a nonissue at your school? Is collaboration always the best idea? When is it not?

We've all seen the go-in-my-room-and-shut-the-door kind of educators. What are the benefits of this kind of teacher? What can be the potential drawbacks?

Explain your honest thoughts about your administrators. What concerns or fears do you have about them? How do you plan to address them? What things do you appreciate the most about your administrators? Have you told them?

The parents and caregivers of your students are just as important in the educational experience as your students. In what ways are you ensuring that they feel a part of the process of learning, too? Can you think of more ways you can develop for them to feel even more included and integral to the team?

Give your all, even if
your all's just a little

From beginning to the end,
plus the stuff in the middle

If your aim is excellence,
then the following is true:

The results mean something, but
the work does, too!

CHAPTER 9

Everyone Deserves Your Excellence

You've likely noticed that many of the themes of this book are about allowing your humanity to show and being open and accepting to the full range of humanity expressed by everyone else. At first blush, a chapter on excellence may seem out of step with this let-people-be-people model. After all, it sounds demanding, right? Who among us can just be characteristically excellent? How is that even possible? And better yet, what does excellence even mean?

My simple definition of excellence is this: the work or effort you put into doing something well. Excellence is not necessarily what comes out, but rather, the endeavor it takes to produce it. I tell scholars all the time, "If you truly gave your all studying for that test, don't beat yourself up about the failing grade you received. Yes, if you're able to try something different next time, or try harder, do so; but I'm pleased with your work. You should be, too!"

Have you ever baked something with a parent or a partner and had a blast doing it, only to taste the finished product and quickly spit it out? The time spent doing something together was excellent. The brownies? Not so much. This is precisely my point. Excellence is less about what you can make, and more about the process it takes to make it. The way we do things can mean a lot more than the things that actually get done. This is the bedrock of educator excellence.

Now, can you be a so-called excellent teacher every minute of every school day? Of course not. Based on current societal standards, nobody can. It's impossible! Some days you'll be tired, and that's frowned upon. So, not excellent. Other days, nothing will go as planned, and for some reason, that's your fault. So, not excellent. Sometimes, the results will look like that of a student's failed exam, an F kind of day. That definitely does not feel excellent. But just because it feels like that doesn't mean it *is* like that.

I want to submit to you that giving your all (even if it's giving the little bit you have when you're tired, when plans go awry, or when you score an F) *is you being excellent*. The worth is found in the work, not in the big, red grade circled at the top of the paper. We must abandon this idea that our value as educators comes from the judgment of others. The score on the report card or the evaluation does not tell the whole story. If we have truly given our best, we should rest knowing we have demonstrated excellence.

> The worth is found in the work, not in the big, red grade circled at the top of the paper.

Not So Excellent Moments

Looking back on it, some of my best lessons as a teacher, or rather the greatest lessons I've learned, have come from the absolute dumpster fires I've created while teaching in the classroom.

My third year in the game, I worked with a special education teacher whom I just didn't care for as a person. She wasn't too fond of me either. Mrs. Jones had a real know-it-all and holier-than-thou personality, and we just didn't see eye to eye on much. One day, she needed to come into my room to observe a student in her care, so we set a time for right after lunch.

Rookie mistake.

Those fourth graders tore me up after coming back from lunch and recess! First, the SMART Board stopped working. Next, I didn't have anything substantial prepared for a just-in-case moment. Nobody was listening to a single word I said, and it's almost as if they collectively planned to turn on me that day. Kids were arguing across the room with each other over the silliest things, it was loud, and worst of all, the classroom was so freaking hot. Lessons, classroom management, and all signs of order went right out the window we had opened to get some fresh air from. It was so embarrassing, especially since it was happening in front of a person I knew didn't like me. In fact, things got so bad that Mrs. Jones wasn't even able to assess the student she came to observe. I know for a fact she left my classroom thinking I didn't belong anywhere near a school. Excellent? *Stop it*! That day, I looked like hot garbage.

But even in this, my cringiest moment as a teacher, I tried to extract a lesson. What could I possibly learn from this experience? How could I make sense of the work and not just the results?

Every lesson after that, I knew I would have to be double and triple prepared. Never again would I go into a situation relying on a piece of equipment without checking it beforehand and without having a backup plan.

To finish that story, Mrs. Jones eventually visited another time, and we never talked about that debacle, but I made sure to learn from it.

The biggest thing I learned was that I must be humble enough to understand that things won't always go my way. I won't always teach rockstar lessons that blow everyone's mind, and that's OK!

Excellence comes from being present in the moment, reflective on how you handled it, and receptive to criticism and feedback as you move forward. It's learning to do things at a deeper level, or to do them differently once the initial experience has passed. Yes, I failed at teaching that day in front of Mrs. Jones, but because I am always growing in excellence, I am a better teacher today due to that experience. Every student deserves this level of ever-growing excellence from both you and me.

Your Favorite Person Is Observing

If your favorite celebrity were to walk into your classroom on a random Tuesday morning, how would things play out? I mean, after all your screaming, sweating, or hyperventilating was over, what would the day look like? Would you phone it in and carry on like any other regular day, or would you put your best foot forward as an educator to dazzle the star in front of you? I'm guessing the latter.

Or what if your beloved grandmother made a special appearance? After showering you with kisses and handing you a tinfoil-wrapped bowl of her famous chili that she brought for lunch—how would class go? I imagine that on this day, you would showcase some of the best lessons you'd ever taught! Your energy would be through the roof! Why? Cause Nana's in the house! And everybody wants to impress Nana!

That's what excellence is. It's performing like your biggest fan is in the room, even if they're not. Excellence is giving your all to impress someone, even if that someone is just yourself. It's not fear based or arising out of a concern that you'll be judged and found wanting. It's not about Big Brother or Santa Claus or even the principal watching over you, jotting critical notes down or adding you to the naughty list.

Nope. *You* are the grader. *You* are the judge. *You* know what you're most capable of giving, and excellence is the constant desire to give just that! Excellence means being honest about what you have to offer at any given moment and then providing that. Excellence is more about integrity than ability. Therefore, the question I often ask myself is, What will I be today, and how will I perform even when no one is watching me? Another is, Am I being the educator I'd want for my own children? I must honestly answer those questions then move accordingly.

Is Beyoncé sitting at my round table while I teach my geography lesson?

Unfortunately, not. But I'm going to teach as if she was!

Cause, I mean, "*Who run the world? Girls!*"

What about Results?

You might be thinking to yourself, "All that excellence stuff sounds great, but my job depends on my results. So, now what?" Well, let's talk about that.

> Excellence means being honest about what you have to offer at any given moment and then providing that.

Have you ever been in a data meeting where all the teachers are reviewing their students' scores from the past month or quarter? It sucks. A range of numbers and bright colors are on full display, and teachers find themselves in the proverbial hot seat. The judgment in the room is as thick as those papers I need to put in the gradebook before the semester ends.

The way one of my old schools had it set up was like a visual stoplight: green meant the kids were where they needed to be; yellow meant they were approaching understanding of various standards; and red meant I was failing them as a teacher—or at least that's what it felt like that color was saying.

"It's not fair," I'd think to myself. "I taught my freaking heart out and those kids definitely learned something! I've seen them grow and give so much of themselves over time. That should count for something, right?! And because some kids aren't great test takers, that's my fault? And wait, am I the one to blame for the students who were goofing around all week while I taught this unit? That doesn't seem fair!"

It's not. The results of our work, while certainly important, do not tell the whole story. The data is not more important than the doing. The Excel sheet or the Word document is not more important than the work. They are equally important. That said, being rated on one data point stinks. And if you've ever sat in one of these meetings, you know this feeling all too well.

Get Rid of Results?

So, does this mean we should stop caring about results altogether? I say no, mainly because it's not probable or practical. Our society is consumed with output. Who won? What was the score? What were their sales? How many people showed up to the event? Everything is about stats! Even in the education world, funding for schools can be about stats, too. In many cases, the amount of money a school receives is tied directly to what teachers and students can do or how they performed on a standardized test.

This demand for results is why many educators feel forced to teach to the test instead of teaching to and from the heart. The humanity of it all gets stripped away. The options seem to be either to experience the joys of teaching and learning *or* to aim for your scholars to score well on an examination. Put bluntly: focus on the results, or else.

The unfortunate reality is that the demand for results isn't going anywhere. Thus, it would be careless of me to advocate for educators to give them up. We must keep them in mind and stay cognizant of our responsibilities. It is our job to teach.

However, I'm strongly suggesting that we assign more weight and significance to the story being told between the lines. Let's care about the end, for sure, but let's also care about the stuff in the middle.

Excellence and Perfection Are Not Synonymous

As we've discussed, excellence is the ongoing attitude to give your best effort in the moment. But I'm not saying that being excellent is the same as being perfect. It's not. And don't let the glitz and glam of social media fool you—no matter how curated one's profile or life is, nobody has it all together all the time. No one is perfect.

More than likely, the Joneses—a.k.a. that teacher up the hall, a.k.a. the edu-celebrity on your timeline—all have their own difficulties or struggles, some which you might have no idea about. So, when you're feeling less than perfect, remember, even the best teacher you can think of feels that way sometimes, too.

Admittedly, I won't score a one hundred percent every day that I teach out of a 185-day school year. There will be days where my self-assigned teacher grade will be embarrassingly low. That's just me being real. But just because I won't score one hundred percent every day, doesn't mean I won't pass or make an *A* on many days.

I absolutely love the phrase, "You get an *A* for effort." Most people use it as a joke or as an attempt to cut someone down to size after a perceived failure. But I think it's more valuable to use than just as a dig at someone. "You get an *A* for effort" should be championed in the education space because it acknowledges and affirms the work teachers (and their students) put in day in and day out. Principals should state it liberally and mean it. Teacher colleagues should encourage one another with the phrase as often as possible. We need to constantly hear, "Hey, your efforts matter," so that we can start to believe that our efforts truly do matter!

It saddens me that so many educators lose pride in themselves because of how others think of them, whether that's their administrators, the parents of their students, or our society. Others expect perfection, so when teachers are not perfect, they are immediately placed on the chopping block of public opinion. That's nonsense because—news flash—nobody's perfect! And for the record, solid work is solid work. Can't nobody take that away from you! While it may not have been perfect, it has been filled with purpose. Rest in that. That's excellence.

Perfectionism can also be holding yourself to rigid, impossible standards and saying negative things to yourself when you fall short. The research is vast on the negative effects of perfectionism. It causes

> When you read excellence, please do not read perfection.

stress, anxiety, and, counterintuitively, less productivity. "Findings suggest that perfectionism dimensions are distinct in creating a dysregulated stress process."[1] When you read excellence, please do not read "perfection." Read "offering your best, whatever that is in the moment."

Excellence Can Be Developed

An objection I often hear about my drive for excellence is, "You've been doing this your whole life. It's not that easy for everyone else to just flip a switch and become excellent." I agree. There's not usually just one moment that will change everything, but thankfully, there are a lot of little actions that can be taken to shift how you move going forward.

We do not have to be who we've always been. Excellence can be developed. How? By practicing it in low-stakes situations. When the pressure's not on and the temperature isn't dialed up, that's the perfect time to build your capacity to excel. Excellence is a long game, but it's won in the short term. The victory comes in the momentary and the minutia.

Here's an example of a low-stakes situation in which you can raise your excellence bar. If you're reading a book aloud to your students, be it *Charlie and the Chocolate Factory* or *Macbeth,* immerse yourself in the story. Become Willy Wonka with your movements and in how you say certain words, or do your best Morgan Freeman or Sigourney Weaver impression as the narrator during Shakespeare's most riveting tale! Or say you're doing a classroom chant; scream it out with pride and great energy! Break a sweat doing it! Be big with it! Be bold in it! It is in the

---

[1] Hanna Suh et al., "Perfectionism, Prolonged Stress Reactivity, and Depression: A Two-Wave Cross-Lagged Analysis," *Journal of Rational-Emotive & Cognitive-Behavior Therapy* 42, no. 1 (November 7, 2022): 54–68, https://doi.org/10.1007/s10942-022-00483-x.

regular, boring, commonplace experiences that many overlook where brilliance is bred. These moments matter.

Or what about when you're walking your kids down to the lunchroom or the library? Excellence would be taking those thirty seconds and making them special somehow. Whisper-sing a popular song with them. Narrate the walk while pointing out funny things each kid is doing. Have a math or vocabulary review at the front of the line while everyone's waiting to go into the school assembly or the computer lab. Those are just a few simple ideas to help make a small moment pop.

Whenever my students and I take a field trip, I intentionally position myself in the middle of the bus, smack dab in the mix of everything. This is partially for safety and support purposes, but it's also so that I can play games, sing songs, and give my everything on that forty-five-minute bus ride. Even if you're not the be-in-the-middle-of-everything kind of person, you can still excel in a similar way. Sit in the front of the bus next to the kid who is more reserved or shy and have a conversation with them. It's not just a trip to the museum, it's an opportunity to build and deliver on excellence. We must remember that relationships matter. Excellence is not just expressed in formal, professional ways; it's forged in the informal, sometimes messy moments of everyday life. Even if they are small moments like a bus ride to the museum, any moment could be the most connective point you ever have with a particular student. Use it! Take it seriously! Low stakes do not mean low rewards. There's always a big payoff for intentionally making magic out of the mundane.

Rest Produces Excellence

Another way to develop excellence in ourselves as educators is to rest. One year, I had the privilege of being the keynote speaker for a large education conference in the Midwest. Before I went up to do my thing, the superintendent over all the schools shared a brief word with their staff. They said, "I want you all to know that being tired is not an option." I dang near spit my water out when I heard this. Like, whoa, do you *want* your teachers to absolutely hate you? That's how you do it. I simply could not believe the superintendent had uttered those words to hundreds of educators who had to be exhausted by that time.

The truth of the matter is that being tired *is* an option! Sometimes, it's the only option, and we should all be grateful because, somehow, teachers have continued to push through. Teachers need rest to be at their best. I find it critical to acknowledge the biological fact that being tired shows we are human. And as humans, everything about school, education, and teachers should submit to this reality. We are not robots; we are people. So, it is of the utmost importance to honor people's humanity and serve them by letting them rest. When we don't prioritize rest, we can't prioritize the rest. Everything falls by the wayside when we neglect to take rest along the way.

During my first few years as a classroom teacher, I worked all the time, even when I was away from the school. So much of my time away involved things like grading, writing lessons, and communicating with parents. I thought this was what was required of me. I thought this was what my administrators wanted. "This is just the way things are for teachers," I thought. There was no rest for the weary.

I don't believe I was alone in my thinking. Too many teachers subscribe to the unwritten rules of "Do more" and "Keep going," even if we won't admit to it. There's this cloud of expectations (some given by others, others self-imposed) looming over our heads or tucked in the back of our classrooms that makes us feel like we must always be going, doing, and performing perfectly. Rest, we convince ourselves, goes against the virtue of helping others. How can I help if I'm not there? We think if we slow down, the kids and their families will suffer, when all the while, our own personal children and families suffer by the minute due to us not tending to ourselves. It is a challenging existence we have as educators in this day and age. The grind-don't-stop mentality is grinding us to dust.

But I learned something a few years in: I don't have to work my fingers down to the bone to be considered an effective teacher. I can rest then educate others more efficiently when I return restored from that rest. That is the truth, and I must operate within that truth.

When I worked as a school administrator, I would encourage my staff to take time off or to liberally use their personal days, and I would praise them for doing so. I would literally beg them to leave work at work and focus on what was most important—whether that was themselves, their family, or whatever else was their business and not mine. "The school will still be here when you get back," I would tell them. And I'd say this because I needed them to know that our community was all about care and completely against grind culture. I would also substitute for their classes if there was no one else available to cover.

Great administrators will never be okay with creating and leading work zombies. The walking dead among us do us no good. (Unless you consider brains getting eaten during a zombie apocalypse as good!) Great administrators should lead and empower their people to fill themselves with peace, purpose, and promise. This means encouraging them to rest then providing the time and space for them to do so. There can be no excellence where there has been no rest.

Students Deserve Your Excellence

When you show up as your excellent self, you invite your scholars to do the same. As with anything, modeling is everything. When they see you, they'll try to figure out how to be you, just in their own way. If you're funny, they'll come prepared with the jokes. If you're organized, they'll know you expect things to be kept in order. If you're high energy, they'll be ready to bounce off the walls in your class! So what do you think will happen if you're excellent? Your scholars will strive to be excellent, too! And you'd better believe, they gon' come correct with it.

Ever had a student pretend to be you in class? Jokingly mimic how you walk or move around the room? Or what about a kid who dresses up like you on Twin Day during Spirit Week? Their imitation of you must be flawless because the stakes are high! Why is that? Because everybody knows how Teach walks, talks, and dresses, so Drey or Drew has to get it right or else they won't be getting any laughs or nods of approval from their peers—or from you. Gotta live up to the expectations that have been set!

One of the highest predictors of academic success is teachers' expectations for their students. If they try to dress like you, often they'll try to test like you, as well. As the teacher, we should expect all our students to excel. But keep in mind, our high expectations for them aren't enough to ensure their success. We must also include support for them by way of our example.

I frequently ask myself: Are you giving your everything to those who are watching? Often, it's seeing our efforts that will compel students to give their best efforts. That's what modeling our version of excellence can do. Our way won't always be the best way for each child, but it at least provides them with some way—a basic blueprint. Watching an adult strive for excellence can be the kickstart a kid needs to strive themself.

We Deserve Our Own Excellence

The teacher also benefits from bringing excellence to the classroom. When I worked at the movie theater, I used to clean the auditoriums after each showing. There would be popcorn, food we didn't even serve, dirty diapers, stuff I didn't even want to look at. I had to clean the bathrooms, mop floors, and everything. Nobody really saw me in that job because I floated around in dark theaters every day.

But I saw myself, and being honest about what I could do, I'd spend a full shift of seven or eight hours and say to myself, "I'm going to work hard. I'm going to have integrity. Even though I'm not getting checked on. Even though no one is saying 'Good job, Dwayne.' I'm going to do my best." I'd leave every day feeling proud, knowing that I'd given it my all.

Now multiply that experience by the impact you can make every day as an educator, and imagine how much pride you would feel when you bring your level of excellence! Instead of a dark theater, you're in a bright classroom. Instead of sweeping up popcorn, you're helping kids grow in conflict-resolution skills. It's not the movies, but you are directing and acting in a major production! Will you show up and show out every day? Start now. Lights, camera, action!

Excellence in Every Way

Not everyone wants to achieve the same things, and that's okay. But we can all strive for excellence in our individual efforts. When everyone gives their all, we all have so much more to work with. Schools with these kinds of people will be the schools that are booming and bustling with greatness! Be *that* teacher who gives everything you can in the moment because you know everyone deserves that. That's excellence!

Reflections

How would you define excellence? How do you define excellence as an educator? What are your own personal expectations surrounding your performance? How do the opinions of others factor into the expectations you have for yourself?

___

___

___

How do you respond to failure? How do you respond to the failure of others around you? What steps do you take immediately after dropping the ball or missing the mark? What needs to change about your perspective on failure, or how you process it? Are you more driven by data or the doing?

___

___

___

What would your classroom look and feel like if your favorite person in the world was watching you teach? How can you make every day in your class look and feel like that day? What small steps can be taken toward improvement?

___

___

___

Does perfectionism impact you? Are you tempted to give in to it?

_____
_____
_____
_____

Describe how you rest. What would a perfect day of rest look like for you?

_____
_____
_____
_____

How can you pause and be more reflective about your teaching?

_____
_____
_____
_____

Not all you say will
be accepted,

Not all that is heard
will be received.

But teaching will extend
beyond the classroom,

When you model for scholars
the things you believe.

CHAPTER 10

Teaching beyond the Classroom

When you read the title of this chapter, you may have thought, "Teaching, even when I'm off the clock? No way!" I get you, dear friends, but that's not at all what I mean. Teaching beyond the classroom means expanding your focus to understand that the impact you make goes well beyond the facts and figures discussed in your room. As a teacher, you are helping shepherd whole, important individuals through the journey of personal evolution, so the effects of this work are bound to make waves past your class.

Throughout this book, we've been talking about teaching to the heart. What this means is practicing a pedagogy that keeps humanity front of mind. When we teach our young people how to be better people, this work benefits all people! The heart work we do in schools inevitably spills out and impacts our communities and ultimately the world. That's teaching beyond the classroom.

The question now becomes, How do we do this? How should you structure your teaching so that it advances past the primary educational space? Well, if you work with the concepts and tenets presented in this book, that's a good start.

Secondly, and it's going to sound simple, but you must do your best to make memories that matter. Once a scholar leaves your classroom, the one thing you can guarantee they'll take with them is memories from their experience there. Thoughts of how they were treated, affirmed, and celebrated will stay with them, sometimes forever. Words that were shared with them or said about them will remain in them. This is why it's important for teachers to focus on creating positive moments that are worth remembering. We have to be intentional to do this.

Take a walk down memory lane with me. Don't we all remember that one educator who did something special for us when we were kids? Something that transcended the books we read, or the math problems we worked on. Now, as adults, we can be *that* teacher for the children we serve. When our mind is set on being special for others, what comes about will always be special to others. That's a guarantee!

> When our mind is set on being special for others, what comes about will always be special to others.

Our Little Representatives

Teaching beyond the classroom means that the stuff you've taught inside the classroom bears fruit outside of it. The memory of what you model as an educator in here makes all the difference for the student out there. When you truly consider this in-to-out framework, it will revolutionize how you speak, move, and behave while in the presence of your students because you know that kids are always taking mental, social, and emotional notes. This means the evidence of how you teach, how you serve, and how you love will be broadcast the moment your students leave your shared space. This is why I often encourage educators to "teach like Johnny's mama is sitting in the room" because, ultimately, word of anything, good or bad, is going to make its way back to Johnny's mama!

Whether you like it or not, preschoolers up to high school seniors will be the bona fide ambassadors of the message and methods you use in your classroom. So let's have them deliver messages about the good stuff! This reality should compel every educator to approach kids with tenderness, empathy, and compassion, rather than engaging with pettiness, harshness, or fighting fire with fire. When someone asks students, "Where did you learn to be kind, or to apologize, or to take accountability for yourself?" let's make sure our students can confidently say, "I learned that from my teacher."

Nine Principles of Teaching beyond the Classroom

So, what are the principles to keep in mind to ensure our teaching goes beyond the classroom? I have nine for you to consider:

1. For the Love of It

We don't often talk about love in the educational experience, but it's all up in here. Love is one of the more prevalent principles expressed in education, and teachers know this. It's in our DNA. We give love every day, whether it's by showing up, purchasing extra supplies, or gathering outside resources that will add to a lesson. Teachers show love by sharing a conversation with a student during our prep or sharing some of our food with a kid who says they're hungry during lunch. Love is what brought most of us to teaching and it's what keeps us in the game.

One way I find to keep love front of mind as a teacher is by choosing to love past (or even considering) the things you might think aren't so great about your scholars, your administration, or your school. Love doesn't mean allowing for everything without saying or doing anything, but it does mean finding ways to mutually work out all things.

Yes, something happened, but is there a way we can work through it? How can we learn from it together? That's love talking! It's about being asset-minded instead of working from a place of deficit. It's the difference between saying, "You're late," and "I'm so glad you're here." That's love.

I showed my students love when I taught during the pandemic. In October of 2020, my wife (also a teacher at my school) and I had still never met the fourth-grade students we taught. We'd never seen these kids in person. In the lead-up to Halloween, we got a list of all our students' home addresses. We both dressed up as medical professionals so we could wear masks (great idea, Wifey!), and we made signs that said, "Happy Halloween from Mr. and Mrs. Reed." Another one read, "Trick or treat. Keep six feet. You're the kids we love to teach!" We sanitized our hands thoroughly, made individual bags of candy, drove to all their houses, one by one, and rang the doorbell. We'd step back six feet and wait for them and their parents to come to the door.

Man! We got the gamut of reactions! Everything from, "How do you all know where I live?" to parents who wanted to ask us in. (We declined, for everyone's safety). But we got overwhelming appreciation for our efforts. Everyone was craving human connection by that point. Everyone just wanted to feel loved.

One grandma came to the door and said, "You're the couple my grandbaby can't stop talking about." I overhear y'all on the computer every day and what you all are doing. Bless your souls, you're making a change in my baby's life."

That day stands out as a highlight during a challenging time. That was a moment when we decided that we weren't going to let the pandemic run us. It was the day we said, "Yes, we're in this sucky situation, but we are going to get to know our kids. They are going to know that they are loved."

This book is all about re-humanizing the educational experience, and few days stand out as better examples than that one. I know we weren't alone in our desire to connect in unique ways. I saw tons of videos of educators doing similar things, showing up at houses, driving by shouting affirmations from their car, bringing a large whiteboard and doing math in front of their students' houses. Be *that* teacher who does whatever they can to show and share the love for their students.

2. I've Got the Joy, Joy, Joy, Joy

The next value educators should focus on is joy. The joy we bring into the classroom can be contagious and, as we've been discussing, is taken outside of the school right by our kids. The stuff that gets us going usually gets them going, too! Why? Because kids love to root for *that* teacher! In many ways, a win for us is also a win for them.

When teachers get engaged or married, students celebrate. When teachers announce a pregnancy, the kids celebrate and start throwing out potential baby names, of course. When teachers get a dog or a new car, or even a fresh haircut, their students can't help but to compliment them and celebrate. Classrooms are filled with joy when educators give their students opportunities to celebrate joy with them. Simply put, our scholars can be moved to joy when we share our own!

This should go both ways, though. When thinking of our kids, we must look for ways to big them up, too, and to join in on their joyfulness. One of my favorite ways to multiply this experience for my students is by showing up at events they invite me to outside of school.

During my student-teaching, one of my scholars, Carlos, told me he loved playing soccer. I asked him when his next game was, then I surprised him by pulling up to the field on that Saturday morning. I had made a sign for him that read, "Go, Carlos," complete with a badly drawn soccer ball. (It's the thought that counts!). It turned out Carlos was phenomenal at soccer, and upon scoring a goal, he ran up to me and gave me the biggest hug! He wanted his educator to celebrate with him and to join him in his joy. He was excited his parents were rooting him on, of course, but the treat of seeing his teacher there made him feel especially joyful. The strong relationship I built with Carlos and his family began that rainy Saturday morning on a soccer field. Be *that* teacher who does everything they can to celebrate their joy and produce it in others.

3. Break Me off a Peace

The next principle I set my mind on daily in the classroom is peace. Don't we all just want peace? For me, I find it in recognizing that I can't control everything. This means focusing on what I can control and releasing the rest. Peace is a mindset we must work to maintain—an ongoing journey, not necessarily a destination. When teachers demonstrate peace when things go awry or a level of peace that simply doesn't make sense given the circumstances, many kids watching will see this and want that for themselves.

It's like when you're on an airplane and there's bad turbulence, but you peek over at the flight attendants to see what they're doing. You're looking for direction on how you should feel during a scary moment. So, when you see them laughing and carrying on as if nothing is the matter, you begin to feel a certain peace rush over you. Our students can experience this same phenomenon in the classroom with us.

When a school event gets canceled or an assembly gets pushed back, leaving everyone all riled up, how do you respond? If the lunch schedule is thrown off or an unexpected fire drill puts all well-laid plans into chaos, how do you respond? Teachers should model peace in the classroom so that when stuff happens outside of the classroom and outside of anyone's control, our scholars will know how they should respond. Be *that* teacher who gives kids a piece of some peace.

4. Patience, Young Grasshopper

Next on the list is patience. The world and the roadways would be much better places if more people practiced patience. There is plenty of time throughout a school year to teach your kids how to wait appropriately, so my recommendation is to start teaching patience early on.

Whether we're asking for them to wait patiently in line before entering the school library or requesting their silence for a few moments while everyone is counted on the school bus, teachers should use everyday scenarios to help kids grow in their ability to be patient. Be explicit in your language about this:

"We need to wait because sometimes others need a little extra time to get things together."

"We're going to be patient here because wouldn't we want someone to be patient with us?"

"Think of all the cool observations we can make while we wait!"

A proper view of patience develops understanding or an empathy for others, and this development helps destroy selfishness. When kids choose to wait their turn on the playground or wait for their classes' slot during picture day, their understanding of existing in a shared space and time with others grows. It's an equity issue. No one person deserves public goods sooner than the next. Instead of wanting to go first, patience produces a heart that looks to serve first.

When the movie *Black Panther* came out, I organized a field trip for our students to see it. It was gonna be so dope! Black excellence on full display! The trouble was that the movie theater messed up our school's viewing time, and there was no room for our kids when we got there. Everybody knows you only get a certain amount of time with a school bus, and it looked like the day was going to be ruined. But my kids were patient. They sat inside a theater showing *Jumanji: Welcome to the Jungle*, while we tried to figure out a solution. They waited without complaint, hopeful for a good resolution. In the Bible, this notion of peaceful patience is known as suffering well.

> Instead of wanting to go first, patience produces a heart that looks to serve first.

The employees at the theater worked hard to squeeze us into another showing of *Black Panther*, and they refunded all of the payments students had made for snacks as a sign of good will. That day, I was blessed to have my scholars experience the lesson of how patience literally pays off. Be *that* teacher who takes the time to show their students how to be patient.

5. Build 'Em with Kindness

No conversation of teaching beyond the classroom would be complete without a passage on kindness. Kindness is one of the world's greatest resources, and those who commit to being kind are some of the world's greatest people. Kindness in the classroom can be as simple as listening intently. It can be befriending someone who looks like they need a homie. We can inspire students to be kind by asking them to look for ways to encourage their peers or to highlight the good they see in them.

But kindness isn't only about children. It's about treating your colleagues the way you'd like to be treated. Not just nicely, but the optimum gold standard of treatment. Kindness can be presented in the way we react or respond to parents or caregivers who haven't been so kind to us. Kids are watching when we're interacting with other adults, so let's be intentional to give them something great to see! Beyond modeling it, we can also talk about the power of kindness in our classrooms and how it fits into building a better world. Students should be encouraged to show kindness no matter who they're with or where they are. Be *that* teacher who shines bright in this dark world because of their kindness.

6. Goodness Gracious!

Related to kindness is goodness. What is goodness? Some describe it as a life characterized by deeds motivated by righteousness and a desire to be a blessing to others. That is goodness at its core. It's wanting to give of yourself and to others without concern for the favor being returned. It's about not being stingy with the good you have. It's about sharing from your place of abundance or wealth. To me, goodness means I've been blessed to be a blessing. I don't want it to end with me, I want it to multiply into the lives of others. It means you, as the teacher, are fighting for others politically and socially. Goodness is simply about just being a decent, altruistic human being.

Whenever possible, I identify opportunities to build empathy for others and encourage goodness. One such moment came up while I had taken a handful of students on a weekend field trip. As we walked past someone who looked to be experiencing homelessness and was panhandling for money, a few of my kids made rude remarks such as, "Go get a job," or "Ain't nobody finna give you no money, bro!" I waited until we'd passed the person, then pulled them to the side. I said, "That's a human being we just walked by. That's a whole person, someone who was born to a mother or a father, just like you. Next time, how about you look them in the eye and say something good. That's the kind of person I know you all can be." I was stern, but I needed them to know that bullying someone, even an adult, is never OK.

Our path took us past the same man on the way back. This time, my students were going out of their way to be kind and show goodness. "I got some change," one of them called out, offering it to him. Someone else gave him an unopened McDonald's cheeseburger from our recent restaurant visit.

This lesson was twofold: you need to be looking for ways to be empathetic, and if you don't do things right the first time, you can always do better the next time. That's the greatness of goodness! Be *that* teacher who is devoted to bringing about the good this world needs now.

7. Faithful in the Little

I desire to have faithful people around me. I enjoy being around those who follow through, as it creates a feeling of safety and security. When my administrator comes through on something they've committed to, I value that, and my respect for them grows. When my colleagues promise to help me complete the interesting task my principal assigned then actually do it, I feel supported and affirmed. But faithfulness doesn't have to stop with just the adults.

Wanting a classroom built on faithfulness is a good desire. We should aspire to have the shared educational space abounding in consistency and dependability. There's nothing wrong with encouraging your students to be faithful in all they do and helping them to develop the discipline to do those things. Hold your students to a high standard of faithfulness and support them as they go to live up to that standard.

There's a saying on posters in schools around the country which reads, "Reach for the stars!" I think that's great encouragement, but what if we focused first on pushing our students to reach the end of that book they started? What if we motivated them to consider that reaching the stars, while possible, will be made more probable when they reach their daily goals and follow through on their regular commitments consistently? "How about we turn in that assignment I gave last week, sir." Then, celebrate them when they keep to their word and accomplish their work!

Faithfulness starts with us, though. As the adult in the room, faithfulness means sticking with a new routine just long enough to see if it catches on and not throwing your hands up at the first sign of trouble. Run with it for a couple of days. Then, if it doesn't work out, you can move onto something different in a week or so. Faithfulness could even look like following through with the consequences you've previously discussed. The follow-through is what matters most here. When kids know that you're going to do what you say, you build a sense of trust with them. At that point, they'll believe what you say when you say it.

Even though we may not see the result of all our efforts in our lifetime, we still have the responsibility to be faithful to our word and our mission. If you've been teaching for a while now, how many times has a kid come back to you years later to let you know what a difference you made with an action or a phrase you may not even remember uttering? That's the reward of faithfulness! Be *that* teacher who sees things through and whose students know they can always depend on.

8. Let Gentleness Lead

To make sure your teaching extends beyond the classroom, when you can, look to how you can approach your job with gentleness. Proverbs 15:1 says, "A soft answer turns away wrath." Imagine how my kids would at least attempt to give a soft answer to their peers or their siblings if they experience you giving them a soft answer regularly. Read the room and respond accordingly. Be chill under the pressures of classroom issues and demonstrate the strength of self-restraint. Meet the monsters of the moment with meekness.

The big piece about gentleness isn't in what you say but, more so, how you say it. When we, as the adult and educator, are self-aware and live in that awareness, our students become more self-aware. Self-awareness comes from a place of compassion. In compassion, I choose to discover more about myself so that this knowledge can inform how I treat others. Teachers have a lot of power in children's lives, so it is incumbent upon us to demonstrate that power carefully and in a way that serves them. We are often viewed as giants in the lives of our little ones (or our bigger ones), so why not be seen as *gentle* giants?

One great example of letting gentleness lead happened during a mentorship program I started at my school. The eighth graders were paired with second graders as buddies, and they read and talked together about life, school, and everything else. There was one second grader, George, who was small for his age and struggled with hearing. I made sure to pair him with an eighth grader, Mike, who was the biggest kid in the school. At just thirteen, Mike was already six foot, four inches tall; but he was a big teddy bear of a kid. This giant Black child, whom the world might deem as scary, whom the second grader might see as scary, exhibited such caring and such gentleness that George came to adore him and love his interactions with him. It took a little coaching with Mike on how to be aware of himself and his size and power and how to use it to be gentle with George. But it paid dividends not just with those two children but with everyone who witnessed their interactions and the great power of gentleness. Be *that* teacher who recognizes their strength and uses it to protect and provide for the people in front of them.

9. Control What You Can—Yourself

Lastly, practicing self-control will undoubtedly make a tremendous impact on your scholars beyond the classroom. I consider self-control to be cultivating the discipline to make moves that will benefit yourself and others. It means having the ability to say no, not right now, or even saying yes to yourself and sticking to that decision. Self-control could either be a denial of self or an acceptance of the truest version of self, depending on the situation. And there are many times in the classroom where the need for self-control is evident.

One example that occurs to me is that of swearing. As kids get older, many of them decide that swear words can make things more fun or spicy when they communicate with their peers. As the teacher, instead of approaching them from my high horse, from a stance of moral superiority, or from a place of judgment, I simply challenge them to practice self-control. I don't say, "Stop doing that because I think it's wrong." I say, "That kind of language is not appropriate for this space." I remind them that how their parents or caregivers let them speak is their business, but here in this workspace, protecting everyone is my business.

As an educator, I'm the leader. Being the leader doesn't mean being the dictator, but it does mean I must use and express my power well. That said, I get to decide if foul language; crude talk; or racist, discriminatory, or derogatory comments have a place in my classroom—and they don't!

After communicating my expectations for students concerning language in the classroom, they have the choice of if and how they'll live up to that expectation. I'm calling for them to watch what they say and to control their mouth. I'm giving them the chance to resist the urge to do whatever they feel like doing in the moment and to accept the challenge of doing what best benefits themselves and others in the long run.

And in the best case, their decision to practice self-control will be made in other ways even outside of the classroom. Those who exercise self-control are truly the ones in control. Be *that* teacher who wants nothing more than for your students to feel in control of their life.

Beyond

Teaching beyond the classroom means you're not teaching to the test, but you are teaching to the test of life. The things we offer our kids are more caught than taught. What they see, they will do. They're soaking up everything we do and say and taking that out into the world. Teaching beyond the classroom doesn't come from a book. It comes from the heart. There can be no rebuttal to, "We want more kind people." No one can object to patient and empathetic kids. When you approach your work as a teacher focused on the development of your students as people, you will be truly unstoppable. You will be *that* teacher.

Reflections

Which of the nine principles are you strongest at or best in demonstrating? Love, joy, peace, patience, kindness, goodness, faithfulness, gentleness, or self-control? Why are those your strengths?

Think about a time when you modeled one of the principles for your scholars. What happened, and how did your kids respond?

Which of the nine principles of teaching beyond the classroom do you struggle with the most? Why do you think so?

If you could leave your scholars with one thing that they could take with them after being in your class (besides academics), what would that be and why?

Outro

Every day when you wake up, you're faced with a choice: you can either be the teacher carrying out your lessons, doing just enough to get by; or you can be *that* teacher—the one who adds a little extra sauce to the pot. The one who makes a difference, no matter how small, wherever you go. The decision needs to be made every day, even before you get out of bed in the morning. And the good news is that you can start this practice right now, even if you haven't before.

In the chapters you've read, you've gotten tools to take your teaching to the next level. To humanize your work for your students, your colleagues, and yourselves. Now, here are some suggestions for how those concepts might look in action on a typical day of school. Everyone is different, so you'll want to adapt these to your own strengths and skills and, of course, your own circumstances. But take a minute to imagine this day of school with me.

It's 6:00 a.m. and you roll out of bed, excited for the day. You've got your lessons prepared, and you're eager to share some cool stuff with your scholars. It's all mapped out, but not set in stone because sometimes you just have to go with the flow. Sometimes you just need to see how the kids are rockin' with it.

Today, you are going to be *that* teacher.

You grab the lunch you've packed, plus a bag of goodies you've put together to add some fun to your instruction, then you start your walk to school. On your way, a child who is usually quiet in your class hangs out a car window and yells your name, looking clearly delighted to see you out in the wild. You wave and make a mental note to ask him later if he wants to be a helper on an upcoming task. Some kids just need to be seen in different ways at different moments, and you're always on the lookout for those kinds of opportunities to see them.

You keep this front of mind, always, because in education relationships matter.

As you get near the school, you say "What's up," to the kids who got dropped off early. Whether they're pre-kindergarteners or high schoolers, you let them know you're excited to see them. If you teach high school, when you see a kid parking their car, you give them a quick head nod or compliment their ride. Once inside the building, you pop into the gymnasium to take a couple of shots at the hoop or you might jump rope with the younger kids. Or, if you see the middle schoolers doing social media dances for their phones, you know it's okay to put your bagel down and make a cameo appearance or offer to hold the camera for them. "We see you with the angles," they cheerfully say.

You pull aside two to three scholars and ask, "Hey, would y'all like to help me?" The answer is often yes because they'd rather do that than just wait in the hallway or the cafeteria for school to start. Whether it's going to the office to get the copies you just made or helping put papers and supplies on each desk, they appreciate getting that one-on-two (or one-on-three) time by assisting you. While you're working together, you're storing in your mind the things each student says to you so you can use it later. Maybe their brother is coming home from college and they're excited about it, so you make a note to talk about colleges, universities, and especially HBCUs in class later. You know your words matter, and your scholars' words matter too, so you make it your business to be *that* teacher who makes relationships the number one priority.

As a teacher who operates in this educational climate, you know that the data matters, of course. But you make sure to focus on the data that really matters.

Yes, numbers mean something. In most school environments, you and your scholars will be judged on test scores and other such data. It's pretty awful. But, for you, as *that* teacher, what matters just as much as data is the information about your kids and all the things they're willing to tell you. Whether it's during the morning meeting, advisory at the end of the day, home room, or study hall, you know that the stuff your students tell you and the conversations you overhear are where you're getting your cues about their social-emotional learning and their lives. You also know the data doesn't mean anything unless you apply it. What good is treasure if you don't spend it, invest it, or share it?

Maybe your scholars are of an age where it makes sense to start with a journal question. It can be outside of the box or off the wall. But you're looking to draw them in so you can hear their thinking. Because you're *that* teacher, you know that asking those questions is crucial.

When you have that relational data, this lets you personalize your pedagogy. Maybe you intuit that, today, it might be best for some scholars to work individually, while others work in different stations. Older students may be on their laptops or tablets. Perhaps you've assigned some reversed instruction. As the educator, it's not solely about what you're trying to teach them, it's also about what they've shown you about *how* you can teach them. You're always tinkering with the delivery of that instruction.

As always, you know you've got to do you, fam.

As the day gets going, maybe you've got your music blasting, if that's who you are. You're opening up to your scholars about who you are as a human being. You're being you, the person you'd be outside the classroom.

Because kids are always watching, you're authentically you in your speech and your demeanor. For me, Mr. Reed, it means being up on the table, joyfully in someone's face, hyped up while we're doing a chant, when I'm singing a song, or when we're transitioning. That's me. But what's you? Whatever communicates that you, as the teacher, are the asset, that's what you give your students. You know that your presence adds value and when you present your truest self, that's icing on the cake.

You're sharing your heart and your personal stories. Perhaps you make a connection from a text that you're reading, sharing a connection to your life. If you're doing a math lesson, you put things into the word problems that draw from your own experiences.

As *that* teacher, you know "Do You" doesn't mean "Do more." It means *be* you. However you show up in the most authentic way, that is the way to go.

Just like you are doing your best to be you, you also gotta let kids be kids.

When you're *that* teacher, the one who makes a big impact on your scholars' lives, you keep at the forefront of your mind that it's crucial to respond to kids in a way that's empathetic to them, in a way that meets with them compassion. Every time you're faced with a crossroads and you need to make a decision about how to react, you lean on the side of remembering that kids are kids.

If your students are a little too loud while you were playing a game, it's no big deal. The world won't come crashing down just because it's a little too loud. As long as you're all safe in there, you lean into the fun part of life. You take your kids outside when the weather breaks. You say, "For this reading lesson, guess where we can read our books? Outside! And after we finish the lesson, ya'll can go play." Because you're child focused, you know that student choice and student voice are so important. You don't always make the choices. Sometimes, they make their own choices, and you know those are the decisions they learn the most from.

You recognize that it doesn't pay to have a strict life at times when you could have some freedom and levity. It's so freeing to just let people be free.

You'll redirect children, if necessary. You'll set the routines in place. But your scholars know they're not going to hear "rules, rules, rules" from you. You remind them of the expectations, but you ask for agreement that serves the interests of the community, not compliance. You're all in this together.

From there, you pause, reflect, and answer the unspoken question your students are always asking: "How do you see me?" You answer this by celebrating their unique racial and cultural differences, and by proving in tangible ways that you view them as people. As humans. Because you're *that* teacher, you place aside your biases and do everything you can to make each individual scholar sitting before you feel seen, valued, and affirmed.

But you also know it takes a team to teach.

It's lunchtime, so you're interacting with the lunch staff, the custodial staff, or maybe the school secretary. You take a moment to talk to the recess coordinator. With a free minute, you call a parent to let them know their child is doing great. Because you're *that* teacher who is not afraid to ask for help, you pop into the principal's office to request support or to make sure they're on board with a field trip your grade band is thinking of taking. And, of course, since kids are key players on this school team, which includes support staff, other teachers, parents, and administrators, you coach them and lovingly hold them accountable, which furthers your relationship. Maybe you step into their music class and sing with them. Or, if they're at lunch, you take a swing through the cafeteria and talk up a table.

Why do you do all this? Because everyone deserves your excellence.

You know that the post-lunch slump can be real. But you also know you have a finite amount of school time with your scholars, so you're not about to let this time slip away without some value. Now, you may read the room and realize that doesn't mean talking about multiplication tables or the science labs right this minute. But it could mean you sharing a video a scholar has shown you and which you've vetted. Or it could be a walk through the halls and out onto the grounds calling out math problems. For little ones, it could be asking how many posters would be on this wall if you took three away. For older ones, it might be word problems based on the items you see. The learning doesn't only have to happen with hands folded, sitting still. When you're bringing your excellence, you're using your imagination, your enthusiasm, and your mental quickness to help kids catch a love of learning.

You hold yourself to a high standard. It started this morning when you opened your eyes and decided that today you were going to be *that* teacher. That doesn't mean that you don't give yourself grace when you're tired or frustrated. You're human. You give all you can in any moment, and you know that fluctuates from day to day, even hour by hour. It's not just in what gets done but also the doing. It's the drive to give your scholars your excellence.

That all comes from a place of the teacher being the lead learner.

Too often, teachers try to create an air of infallibility, like we always know everything. But if what you're looking to create is a love of learning, not the ability to memorize details, then you've got to model that love. If someone asks a question in class to which you don't know the answer, challenge the kids that you'll all go find it together on the spot or that you'll all come ready to discuss it the next day. If a scholar calls you out on a misstep or on a way in which you made them feel bad, even if you didn't mean to, own that. Show them what it looks like to be *that* teacher who apologizes and really means it when you say you'll work to do better. An air of humility and of being a work in progress will help kids be kind to themselves when they recognize the ways in which they still have to grow.

So, as the lead learner, this afternoon, you let your scholars teach you something. Maybe it's the latest viral dance or some new slang. You apologize if you don't get everything just right at first. You show them we are always still growing and learning.

In these and other small ways, you rebel against the norm. Rebelling against the norm of "the teacher is always right" is one small way to teach your scholars that everything is up for debate and reexamination. But there are countless others you can embody every day. Maybe this afternoon, one of your scholars complains about a new school policy they think is unfair. If you hear a ring of truth in their complaint, rather than just upholding the policy, talk over some ways in which the kids might band together to try to get the policy revised or dropped completely. Talk to them about petitions, letters to the principal, and pieces in the school or community newspaper. Rebelling can be easy, like asking why it is that everyone must walk silently and in single file to the bathroom. It could also be big stuff, like teaching kids to start "good trouble" when justice calls for it. Just because something is the norm doesn't mean it's right. You stand up for your beliefs for your sake and teach kids to stand up for theirs.

When you think about rebelling against the norm, that's a good jumping off point to think about the ways your teaching extends beyond the classroom. You're not only helping to shape ninth graders, or whatever grade you're teaching. You're helping to build citizens, future mothers and fathers, future business leaders and politicians, future clergy and teachers. This work will expand your reach. Rather than focusing on what you're going to do during the last period of the day, you ask yourself what impactful lesson you can leave kids with for tomorrow. You ask yourself if there's a way you can serve the kids even after school is done. Whether it's email office hours after school or creating a classroom party as a reward for finishing up a particularly hard lesson, think of yourself not just as the teacher for the day but as *that* teacher who will help shape this year and, maybe for a handful of kids, even beyond that.

Being *that* teacher is not necessarily about being the teacher kids remember (although of course it feels nice when they do). It's about being an adult in their lives who shows them what's possible, by example and by word. It's about imagining the teacher you wish you'd had during a particularly challenging year of your life and striving to be that person. You can never know who precisely needs to hear what you share from your genuine self at any given moment. It won't be magic and rainbows for every single scholar every day you're in that classroom. But know, even if you weren't the best teacher today, chances are you were still someone's favorite.

When you show up authentically, all out, not afraid that you might be bending the rules or that you're being too much, you're going to be *that* teacher for the kids who need you. And, even for the ones that think you may not quite be their flavor, you're going to show them what it's like to *do you*, be unapologetically yourself, and be joyful and real in the process. And what more can we want for kids than for them to learn how to unapologetically be themselves?

So, go out there and be *that* teacher. The world is waiting for you.

Acknowledgments

Hey Moms, I'm pretty sure I became a teacher because of you, so thank you. To be honest, I never gave education a single thought until you threw that one phenomenal teacher book my way—changed the whole trajectory of my life! At that point, I realized that I could make a difference in the world, not just by being a teacher, but by how I chose to show up and show out as a teacher. That moment, along with many others, helped me to see that putting my own style and spin onto the education game was the only way to go. *Be That Teacher* would not exist without you first teaching me. Love you.

Monie—You've been one of my greatest teachers since the eighth grade. From the moment we got seated next to each other in math class, I knew you were the one. Two decades and three kids later, and I'm even more convinced of that fact. As my wife, my friend, and even my co-teacher (at one point) you taught me so much about life and love. Words cannot express what you mean to me and how impactful you've been on this journey. I simply could not be *that* teacher without you. I love you, homie.

M.—A book like this would not have been possible without you. I am eternally grateful for your wisdom, your words, and your willingness to listen to me (even if I was talking a little too much, ha). Thank you for always affirming the good you saw in me as an educator, and for encouraging me to quite literally be *that* teacher. Be blessed, friend.

To my scholars—don't ever let nobody tell you what you are and what you ain't. You get to decide that! You get to be who you want to be, so do that! Y'all have taught me way more than I could have ever taught y'all, and I'm so appreciative of this. I mean this from the bottom of my heart—thank you for showing Mr. Reed how to be *that* teacher. Y'all know what it is.

Teachers—You all are my heroes. I truly believe there's a special place in Heaven set aside for teachers (especially Pre-K and Kindergarten teachers, ha!). Words can do no justice in communicating how thankful I am for teachers getting up every day, working, serving, loving, and keeping this world moving. I am always going to root and fight for us teachers! If you put us up against anybody, the world will see that we are for everybody! Thank you for having this heart. And if you're reading this, thank you for being *that* teacher.

About Dwayne Reed

Dwayne Reed is an author, rapper, proud husband, father, and public school teacher in Chicago. He is in love with his wife and junior-high sweetheart, Simone, and they, along with their children, live happily on the South Side of Chicago.

In 2016, Mr. Reed released his viral music video "Welcome to the 4th Grade," which garnered millions of views and catapulted him into an educational spotlight. Reed believes relationships mean everything in education, and that every child, no matter their race or social status, deserves a fair chance at a quality education. His message to all is one of grace, love, and equity, and his aim is to rehumanize the learning experience for every scholar, everywhere.

Mr. Reed is a highly sought-after keynote speaker for schools, conferences, and educational events. With over 100 keynotes and breakout sessions under his belt, he has reached tens of thousands of educators in person, in print, and through social media. He specializes in delivering inspiration, motivation, and practical strategies that are guaranteed to work from the classroom to the boardroom.

Contact Mr. Reed about speaking engagements via email at dwaynepreed@gmail.com or through social media.

@TeachMrReed

Mr. Reed

More from Dave Burgess Consulting, Inc.

Since 2012, DBCI has published books that inspire and equip educators to be their best. For more information on our titles or to purchase bulk orders for your school, district, or book study, visit DaveBurgessConsulting.com/DBCIbooks.

The *Like a PIRATE*™ Series
Teach Like a PIRATE by Dave Burgess
eXPlore Like a PIRATE by Michael Matera
Learn Like a PIRATE by Paul Solarz
Plan Like a PIRATE by Dawn M. Harris
Play Like a PIRATE by Quinn Rollins
Run Like a PIRATE by Adam Welcome
Tech Like a PIRATE by Matt Miller

The *Lead Like a PIRATE*™ Series
Lead Like a PIRATE by Shelley Burgess and Beth Houf
Balance Like a PIRATE by Jessica Cabeen, Jessica Johnson, and Sarah Johnson
Lead beyond Your Title by Nili Bartley
Lead with Appreciation by Amber Teamann and Melinda Miller
Lead with Collaboration by Allyson Apsey and Jessica Gomez
Lead with Culture by Jay Billy
Lead with Instructional Rounds by Vicki Wilson
Lead with Literacy by Mandy Ellis
She Leads by Dr. Rachael George and Majalise W. Tolan

The EduProtocol Field Guide Series
Deploying EduProtocols by Kim Voge, with Jon Corippo and Marlena Hebern
The EduProtocol Field Guide by Marlena Hebern and Jon Corippo
The EduProtocol Field Guide Book 2 by Marlena Hebern and Jon Corippo
The EduProtocol Field Guide Math Edition by Lisa Nowakowski and Jeremiah Ruesch
The EduProtocol Field Guide Primary Edition by Benjamin Cogswell and Jennifer Dean
The EduProtocol Field Guide Social Studies Edition by Dr. Scott M. Petri and Adam Moler
The EduProtocol Field Guide ELA Edition by Jacob Carr

Leadership & School Culture
Beyond the Surface of Restorative Practices by Marisol Rerucha
Change the Narrative by Henry J. Turner and Kathy Lopes
Choosing to See by Pamela Seda and Kyndall Brown
Culturize by Jimmy Casas
Discipline Win by Andy Jacks
Educate Me! by Dr. Shree Walker with Micheal D. Ison
Escaping the School Leader's Dunk Tank by Rebecca Coda and Rick Jetter
Fight Song by Kim Bearden
From Teacher to Leader by Starr Sackstein
If the Dance Floor Is Empty, Change the Song by Joe Clark
The Innovator's Mindset by George Couros
It's OK to Say "They" by Christy Whittlesey
Kids Deserve It! by Todd Nesloney and Adam Welcome
Leading the Whole Teacher by Allyson Apsey
Let Them Speak by Rebecca Coda and Rick Jetter
The Limitless School by Abe Hege and Adam Dovico
Live Your Excellence by Jimmy Casas
Next-Level Teaching by Jonathan Alsheimer
The Pepper Effect by Sean Gaillard

Principaled by Kate Barker, Kourtney Ferrua, and Rachael George
The Principled Principal by Jeffrey Zoul and Anthony McConnell
Relentless by Hamish Brewer
The Secret Solution by Todd Whitaker, Sam Miller, and Ryan Donlan
Start. Right. Now. by Todd Whitaker, Jeffrey Zoul, and Jimmy Casas
Stop. Right. Now. by Jimmy Casas and Jeffrey Zoul
Teach Your Class Off by CJ Reynolds
Teachers Deserve It by Rae Hughart and Adam Welcome
They Call Me "Mr. De" by Frank DeAngelis
Thrive through the Five by Jill M. Siler
Unmapped Potential by Julie Hasson and Missy Lennard
When Kids Lead by Todd Nesloney and Adam Dovico
Word Shift by Joy Kirr
Your School Rocks by Ryan McLane and Eric Lowe

Technology & Tools
50 Things to Go Further with Google Classroom by Alice Keeler and Libbi Miller
50 Things You Can Do with Google Classroom by Alice Keeler and Libbi Miller
50 Ways to Engage Students with Google Apps by Alice Keeler and Heather Lyon
140 Twitter Tips for Educators by Brad Currie, Billy Krakower, and Scott Rocco
Block Breaker by Brian Aspinall
Building Blocks for Tiny Techies by Jamila "Mia" Leonard
Code Breaker by Brian Aspinall
The Complete EdTech Coach by Katherine Goyette and Adam Juarez
Control Alt Achieve by Eric Curts
The Esports Education Playbook by Chris Aviles, Steve Isaacs, Christine Lion-Bailey, and Jesse Lubinsky
Google Apps for Littles by Christine Pinto and Alice Keeler
Master the Media by Julie Smith
Raising Digital Leaders by Jennifer Casa-Todd
Reality Bytes by Christine Lion-Bailey, Jesse Lubinsky, and Micah Shippee, PhD

Sail the 7 Cs with Microsoft Education by Becky Keene and Kathi Kersznowski
Shake Up Learning by Kasey Bell
Social LEADia by Jennifer Casa-Todd
Stepping Up to Google Classroom by Alice Keeler and Kimberly Mattina
Teaching Math with Google Apps by Alice Keeler and Diana Herrington
Teaching with Google Jamboard by Alice Keeler and Kimberly Mattina
Teachingland by Amanda Fox and Mary Ellen Weeks

Teaching Methods & Materials
All 4s and 5s by Andrew Sharos
Boredom Busters by Katie Powell
Building Strong Writers by Christina Schneider
The Classroom Chef by John Stevens and Matt Vaudrey
The Collaborative Classroom by Trevor Muir
Copyrighteous by Diana Gill
CREATE by Bethany J. Petty
Ditch That Homework by Matt Miller and Alice Keeler
Ditch That Textbook by Matt Miller
Don't Ditch That Tech by Matt Miller, Nate Ridgway, and Angelia Ridgway
EDrenaline Rush by John Meehan
Educated by Design by Michael Cohen, The Tech Rabbi
Empowered to Choose: A Practical Guide to Personalized Learning by Andrew Easton
Expedition Science by Becky Schnekser
Frustration Busters by Katie Powell
Fully Engaged by Michael Matera and John Meehan
Game On? Brain On! by Lindsay Portnoy, PhD
Guided Math AMPED by Reagan Tunstall
Happy & Resilient by Roni Habib
Innovating Play by Jessica LaBar-Twomy and Christine Pinto
Instant Relevance by Denis Sheeran
Instructional Coaching Connection by Nathan Lang-Raad
Keeping the Wonder by Jenna Copper, Ashley Bible, Abby Gross, and Staci Lamb

LAUNCH by John Spencer and A.J. Juliani
Learning in the Zone by Dr. Sonny Magana
Lights, Cameras, TEACH! by Kevin J. Butler
Make Learning MAGICAL by Tisha Richmond
Pass the Baton by Kathryn Finch and Theresa Hoover
Project-Based Learning Anywhere by Lori Elliott
Pure Genius by Don Wettrick
The Revolution by Darren Ellwein and Derek McCoy
The Science Box by Kim Adsit and Adam Peterson
Shift This! by Joy Kirr
Skyrocket Your Teacher Coaching by Michael Cary Sonbert
Spark Learning by Ramsey Musallam
Sparks in the Dark by Travis Crowder and Todd Nesloney
Table Talk Math by John Stevens
Teachables by Cheryl Abla and Lisa Maxfield
Unpack Your Impact by Naomi O'Brien and LaNesha Tabb
The Wild Card by Hope and Wade King
Writefully Empowered by Jacob Chastain
The Writing on the Classroom Wall by Steve Wyborney
You Are Poetry by Mike Johnston
You'll Never Guess What I'm Saying by Naomi O'Brien
You'll Never Guess What I'm Thinking About by Naomi O'Brien

Inspiration, Professional Growth & Personal Development
Be REAL by Tara Martin
Be the One for Kids by Ryan Sheehy
The Coach ADVenture by Amy Illingworth
Creatively Productive by Lisa Johnson
The Ed Branding Book by Dr. Renae Bryant and Lynette White
Educational Eye Exam by Alicia Ray
The EduNinja Mindset by Jennifer Burdis
Empower Our Girls by Lynmara Colón and Adam Welcome
Finding Lifelines by Andrew Grieve and Andrew Sharos
The Four O'Clock Faculty by Rich Czyz
How Much Water Do We Have? by Pete and Kris Nunweiler

P Is for Pirate by Dave and Shelley Burgess
A Passion for Kindness by Tamara Letter
The Path to Serendipity by Allyson Apsey
PheMOMenal Teacher by Annick Rauch
Recipes for Resilience by Robert A. Martinez
Rogue Leader by Rich Czyz
Sanctuaries by Dan Tricarico
Saving Sycamore by Molly B. Hudgens
The Secret Sauce by Rich Czyz
Shattering the Perfect Teacher Myth by Aaron Hogan
Stories from Webb by Todd Nesloney
Talk to Me by Kim Bearden
Teach Better by Chad Ostrowski, Tiffany Ott, Rae Hughart, and Jeff Gargas
Teach Me, Teacher by Jacob Chastain
Teach, Play, Learn! by Adam Peterson
The Teachers of Oz by Herbie Raad and Nathan Lang-Raad
TeamMakers by Laura Robb and Evan Robb
Through the Lens of Serendipity by Allyson Apsey
Write Here and Now by Dan Tricarico
The Zen Teacher by Dan Tricarico

Children's Books
The Adventures of Little Mickey by Mickey Smith Jr.
Alpert by LaNesha Tabb
Alpert & Friends by LaNesha Tabb
Beyond Us by Aaron Polansky
Cannonball In by Tara Martin
Dolphins in Trees by Aaron Polansky
Dragon Smart by Tisha and Tommy Richmond
I Can Achieve Anything by MoNique Waters
I Want to Be a Lot by Ashley Savage
The Magic of Wonder by Jenna Copper, Ashley Bible, Abby Gross, and Staci Lamb
Micah's Big Question by Naomi O'Brien
The Princes of Serendip by Allyson Apsey

Ride with Emilio by Richard Nares
A Teacher's Top Secret Confidential by LaNesha Tabb
A Teacher's Top Secret: Mission Accomplished by LaNesha Tabb
The Wild Card Kids by Hope and Wade King
Zom-Be a Design Thinker by Amanda Fox

Made in the USA
Monee, IL
14 March 2025